Cocos2d-x by Example Beginner's Guide

Second Edition

Unleash your inner creativity and learn how to build great cross-platform 2D games with the popular Cocos2d-x framework

Roger Engelbert

BIRMINGHAM - MUMBAI

Cocos2d-x by Example Beginner's Guide
Second Edition

First published: April 2013

Second edition: March 2015

Production reference: 1240315

Published by Packt Publishing Ltd.
Livery Place
35 Livery Street
Birmingham B3 2PB, UK.

ISBN 978-1-78528-885-2

www.packtpub.com

Cover image by Roger Engelbert (rengelbert@gmail.com)

Credits

Author

Roger Engelbert

Reviewers

Saeed Afshari

Joni Mikkola

Michael Price

Vamsi Krishna Veligatla

Chatchai Mark Wangwiwattana

Commissioning Editor

Akram Hussain

Acquisition Editor

Sam Wood

Content Development Editor

Ritika Singh

Technical Editor

Mrunal M. Chavan

Copy Editors

Sonia Michelle Cheema

Aarti Saldanha

Adithi Shetty

Project Coordinator

Judie Jose

Proofreaders

Simran Bhogal

Maria Gould

Paul Hindle

Indexer

Priya Sane

Production Coordinator

Nitesh Thakur

Cover Work

Nitesh Thakur

About the Author

Roger Engelbert is a game developer, with over 10 years of experience developing online games. He grew up surrounded by video games and thinks of classic, 8-bit, arcade titles as a form of art. He is the author behind the blog *Done With Computers*, which is chock-full of tutorials on game development and design. Roger sincerely hopes to soon live in a world where people of all ages will be given the knowledge and opportunity to experience the joy of building their own games.

I would like to thank the people from Packt Publishing that helped me through the process of writing this book. And above all, my family, who—once again!—had to see a bleary eyed and slightly surly version of myself as I worked on this book long into the night.

About the Reviewers

Saeed Afshari is an independent game developer and a researcher in the area of human-computer interaction. He has published more than 20 titles on the iOS App Store and Google Play under the brand Neat Games, and is focused on developing mobile games for iOS and Android.

He is a member of the Games, Interaction and Novel Interface Technologies (IGNITE) research collective at the University of Luxembourg, working on natural and novel user interfaces, and understanding how people interact with games and how games should interact with people. His current research projects deal with interaction with mobile games, virtual-reality head-mounted displays, and behavior change through serious gaming. He is the game developer for the European Commission project, *LiveCity*, which deals with long distance multiplayer gaming on multitouch tables.

With over 15 years of experience in game development and interactive media, he has built skills in platforms, including OpenGL, DirectX, Unity, Cocos2d-x, and also interaction design for natural user interfaces and virtual reality. He has invented an algorithm to track permanent magnets for use in mobile games, in particular in the form of a magnetic joystick. He is willing to consult and collaborate on creating games and interactive software targeted for education, entertainment, and social networks.

For more information about Saeed and Neat Games, you can contact `pr@neat-games.com`.

Joni Mikkola is currently working on his next mobile game in northern Finland. He keeps his game developing stamina up by training regularly at the gym and eating healthy. Among developing games, he often reads books, plays piano, or bakes buns to keep ideas flowing and mind focused. He constantly keeps challenging the status quo, which in turn helps in learning new ways to create things.

He has developed games for over 4 years professionally mostly for mobile platforms. He targets casual games and focuses on creating simplistic designs. With one game released, he is currently working on his next game, which will be released in early 2015 for Android and iOS platforms. Sometimes he chills by participating in Ludum Dare game contests.

Michael Price has been working in the game industry since 2009. He studied game development at Algonquin College in Ottawa and has always had an interest in technology and programming. He's been playing video games for as long as he can remember and now uses that passion to build fun and exciting games. He has extensive knowledge of building games for the Web and mobile. He has his own website (`http://www.michaelrjprice.com`) that shows all his past and current projects.

I would like to thank my parents for their support, and my girlfriend for always being there for me.

Vamsi Krishna Veligatla is the Director of engineering at Tiny Mogul games, which is the gaming arm of Hike Messenger Pvt Ltd. He was the lead developer on some of the most iconic games such as *Shiva: The Time Bender* and *Dadi vs Jellies* developed at Tiny Mogul Games.

He has a master's degree in computer science from the International Institute of Information Technology, Hyderabad. Previously, he worked at Nvidia Graphics Pvt Ltd, AMD (ATI), and University of Groningen, Netherlands.

> I would like to thank my family for their love and support.

Chatchai Mark Wangwiwattana is a game researcher, designer, and programmer. Currently, he is pursuing a PhD in game-based learning and using video games to improve health. As a freelancer in the gaming industry, Chatchai has been developing games for entertaining and education. *Kraven Manor* was one of the award-winning games at Intel University Showcase, 2014. More information about his works is available at `www.chatchaiwang.com`.

www.PacktPub.com

Support files, eBooks, discount offers, and more

For support files and downloads related to your book, please visit www.PacktPub.com.

Did you know that Packt offers eBook versions of every book published, with PDF and ePub files available? You can upgrade to the eBook version at www.PacktPub.com and as a print book customer, you are entitled to a discount on the eBook copy. Get in touch with us at service@packtpub.com for more details.

At www.PacktPub.com, you can also read a collection of free technical articles, sign up for a range of free newsletters and receive exclusive discounts and offers on Packt books and eBooks.

https://www2.packtpub.com/books/subscription/packtlib

Do you need instant solutions to your IT questions? PacktLib is Packt's online digital book library. Here, you can search, access, and read Packt's entire library of books.

Why subscribe?

- ◆ Fully searchable across every book published by Packt
- ◆ Copy and paste, print, and bookmark content
- ◆ On demand and accessible via a web browser

Free access for Packt account holders

If you have an account with Packt at www.PacktPub.com, you can use this to access PacktLib today and view 9 entirely free books. Simply use your login credentials for immediate access.

Table of Contents

Preface

Cocos2d-x combines the benefits of using one the most popular and test-proven 2D game frameworks out there with the power and portability of C++. So, you get the best deal possible. Not only is the framework built to be easy to use and quick to implement, it also allows your code to target more than one system.

The book will show you how to use the framework to quickly implement your ideas, and let Cocos2d-x help you with the translation of all that OpenGL gobbledygook, leaving you with the fun part: making sprites jump around and hit each other!

There are seven examples of games in this book with two of them being physics-based, using Box2D and one using the Lua bindings and the new Cocos Code IDE. With each example, you'll learn more about the framework and the magical lines that can quickly add particle effects, animations, sounds, UI elements, and all sorts of wonderful things to your games.

Not only this, but you will also learn how to target both iOS and Android devices, and multiple screen sizes.

What this book covers

Chapter 1, *Installing Cocos2d-x*, guides you through the download and installation of the Cocos2d-x framework. It also examines the ins and outs of a basic Cocos2d-x application and deployment to both iOS and Android devices.

Chapter 2, *You Plus C++ Plus Cocos2d-x*, explains the main elements in the framework. It also covers the differences in syntax when developing in C++, and the differences in memory management when developing with Cocos2d-x.

Chapter 3, *Your First Game – Air Hockey*, kick-starts our game development tutorials by using Cocos2d-x to build an air hockey game. You will learn how to load the images for your sprites, display text, manage touches, and add sounds to your game.

Chapter 4, Fun with Sprites – Sky Defense, demonstrates the power of actions in Cocos2d-x, and shows how an entire game could be built with them. It also introduces the concept of sprite sheets and the steps to build a universal application targeting different screen resolutions.

Chapter 5, On the Line – Rocket Through, adds two new elements to our game development toolbox: how to draw primitives, such as lines, curves, and circles, and how to use particle systems to improve the look of our game with special effects.

Chapter 6, Quick and Easy Sprite – Victorian Rush Hour, shows how you can use Cocos2d-x to quickly implement game ideas for further testing and development by rapidly building game prototypes with placeholder sprites. In the game example used for this chapter, you'll also learn how to build a side-scrolling platform game.

Chapter 7, Adding the Looks – Victorian Rush Hour, continues with the project from the previous chapter adding the final touches to the game including a menu and a playable tutorial.

Chapter 8, Getting Physical – Box2D, introduces the popular Box2D API for a physics simulation, guiding you through the process of using Box2D in the development of a pool game. You learn how to create bodies and manage the way they interact with each other.

Chapter 9, On the Level – Eskimo, teaches you how to load external data for game levels, how to store game-related data locally as well as structure your games with multiple scenes. We use a second Box2D game to illustrate these topics, plus a couple of new concepts, such as using the event dispatcher to structure your games better.

Chapter 10, Introducing Lua!, will guide you in the development of a multiplatform match-three game using Lua and the new Cocos Code IDE. You will see how similar the calls are between the C++ version and its Lua bindings and how easy it is to develop a game in Lua.

Appendix A, Vector Calculations with Cocos2d-x, covers some of the math concepts used in *Chapter 5, On the Line – Rocket Through*, in a little more detail.

Appendix B, Pop Quiz Answers, provides answers to the pop quiz available in some chapters.

What you need for this book

In order to run the games developed in this book, you will need Xcode for iOS devices, and Eclipse for Android, as well as the Cocos Code IDE for the Lua game. Although the tutorials describe the development process using Xcode in each chapter of the book, you will see how to import the code in Eclipse and develop and deploy from there.

Who this book is for

You have a passion for games. You may have used Cocos2d already (the Objective-C version of the framework) and are eager to learn its C++ port. Or, you know a little bit of some other C-based language, such as Java, PHP, or Objective-C and you want to learn how to develop 2D games in C++. You may also be a C++ developer already and want to know what all the hoopla about Cocos2d-x is. If you fit any of these scenarios, welcome aboard!

Sections

In this book, you will find several headings that appear frequently (Time for action, What just happened?, Pop quiz, and Have a go hero).

To give clear instructions on how to complete a procedure or task, we use these sections as follows:

Time for action – heading

1. Action 1
2. Action 2
3. Action 3

Instructions often need some extra explanation to ensure they make sense, so they are followed with these sections:

What just happened?

This section explains the working of the tasks or instructions that you have just completed.

You will also find some other learning aids in the book, for example:

Pop quiz – heading

These are short multiple-choice questions intended to help you test your own understanding.

Have a go hero – heading

These are practical challenges that give you ideas to experiment with what you have learned.

Conventions

You will also find a number of text styles that distinguish between different kinds of information. Here are some examples of these styles and an explanation of their meaning.

Code words in text, database table names, folder names, filenames, file extensions, pathnames, dummy URLs, user input, and Twitter handles are shown as follows: "For background music volume, you must use `setBackgroundMusicVolume`."

A block of code is set as follows:

```
CCScene* GameLayer::scene()
{
    // 'scene' is an autorelease object
    CCScene *scene = CCScene::create();

    GameLayer *layer = GameLayer::create();

    scene->addChild(layer);

    return scene;
}
```

When we wish to draw your attention to a particular part of a code block, the relevant lines or items are set in bold:

```
//add score display
_player1ScoreLabel = CCLabelTTF::create("0", "Arial", 60);
_player1ScoreLabel->setRotation(90);
this->addChild(_player1ScoreLabel);
```

Any command-line input or output is written as follows:

```
sudo ./install-templates-xcode.sh -u
```

New terms and **important words** are shown in bold. Words that you see on the screen, in menus or dialog boxes for example, appear in the text like this: "In the dialog box select **cocos2d-x** under the **iOS** menu and choose the **cocos2dx** template."

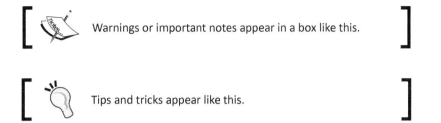

Warnings or important notes appear in a box like this.

Tips and tricks appear like this.

Reader feedback

Feedback from our readers is always welcome. Let us know what you think about this book—what you liked or may have disliked. Reader feedback is important for us to develop titles that you really get the most out of.

To send us general feedback, simply send an e-mail to feedback@packtpub.com, and mention the book title through the subject of your message.

If there is a topic that you have expertise in and you are interested in either writing or contributing to a book, see our author guide on www.packtpub.com/authors.

Customer support

Now that you are the proud owner of a Packt book, we have a number of things to help you to get the most from your purchase.

Downloading the example code

You can download the example code files for all Packt books you have purchased from your account at http://www.packtpub.com. If you purchased this book elsewhere, you can visit http://www.packtpub.com/support and register to have the files e-mailed directly to you.

Downloading the color images of this book

We also provide you with a PDF file that has color images of the screenshots/diagrams used in this book. The color images will help you better understand the changes in the output. You can download this file from https://www.packtpub.com/sites/default/files/downloads/8852OS_GraphicsBundle.pdf.

Errata

Although we have taken every care to ensure the accuracy of our content, mistakes do happen. If you find a mistake in one of our books—maybe a mistake in the text or the code—we would be grateful if you could report this to us. By doing so, you can save other readers from frustration and help us improve subsequent versions of this book. If you find any errata, please report them by visiting http://www.packtpub.com/submit-errata, selecting your book, clicking on the **Errata Submission Form** link, and entering the details of your errata. Once your errata are verified, your submission will be accepted and the errata will be uploaded to our website or added to any list of existing errata under the Errata section of that title.

To view the previously submitted errata, go to https://www.packtpub.com/books/content/support and enter the name of the book in the search field. The required information will appear under the **Errata** section.

Piracy

Piracy of copyrighted material on the Internet is an ongoing problem across all media. At Packt, we take the protection of our copyright and licenses very seriously. If you come across any illegal copies of our works in any form on the Internet, please provide us with the location address or website name immediately so that we can pursue a remedy.

Please contact us at copyright@packtpub.com with a link to the suspected pirated material.

We appreciate your help in protecting our authors and our ability to bring you valuable content.

Questions

If you have a problem with any aspect of this book, you can contact us at questions@packtpub.com, and we will do our best to address the problem.

1
Installing Cocos2d-x

In this chapter, we'll get things up and running on your machine so you can get the most out of the examples in this book. This will include information on downloading the framework and creating a project as well as an overview of the basic structure of a Cocos2d-x application.

I will also point you to some extra tools you should consider getting to help you with the development process, such as tools to build sprite sheets, particle effects, and bitmap fonts. Although these tools are optional, and you can still learn how to use sprite sheets, particles, and bitmap fonts just by following the examples given in this book, you might consider these tools for your own projects.

Things you will learn in this first chapter are as follows:

- ◆ How to download Cocos2d-x
- ◆ How to run your first multiplatform application
- ◆ What the basic project looks like and how to find your way around it
- ◆ How to use the test project as a major reference source

Downloading and installing Cocos2d-x

All the examples in this book were developed in a Mac using Xcode and/or Eclipse. The example in the final chapter uses Cocos2d-x own IDE for scripting. Although you can use Cocos2d-x to develop your games for other platforms using different systems, the examples were built in a Mac and deployed to both iOS and Android.

Xcode is free and can be downloaded from the Mac App store (`https://developer.apple.com/xcode/index.php`), but in order to test your code on an iOS device and publish your games, you will need a developer account with Apple, which will cost you $99 a year. You can find more information on their website: `https://developer.apple.com/`.

For Android deployment, I recommend that you get the Eclipse and ADT bundle from Google, which you can find at `http://developer.android.com/sdk/installing/installing-adt.html`. You will be able to test your games in an Android device for free.

So, assuming you have an Internet connection, let's begin!

Time for action – downloading, downloading, downloading

We start by downloading the necessary SDKs, NDKs, and general bits and bobs:

1. Go to `http://www.cocos2d-x.org/download` and download the latest stable version of Cocos2d-x. For this book, I'll be using version Cocos2d-x-3.4.

2. Uncompress the files somewhere in your machine you can remember later. I recommend that you add all the files we're going to download now to the same folder.

3. Go ahead and download the Code IDE as well. We'll be using this in the last chapter in this book.

4. Then, go to `http://developer.android.com/sdk/installing/installing-adt.html` and download the Eclipse ADT plugin (if you don't have Eclipse or the Android SDK installed, download them at `https://eclipse.org/downloads/` and `http://developer.android.com/sdk/installing/index.html?pkg=tools`, respectively).

 If you have any problems installing the ADT plugin, you will find complete instructions at `http://developer.android.com/sdk/installing/installing-adt.html`.

5. Now, for Apache Ant, go to `http://ant.apache.org/bindownload.cgi` and look for the links to the compressed files, and download the `.zip` one.

6. Lastly, go to `https://developer.android.com/tools/sdk/ndk/index.html` and download the latest version of the NDK for your target system. Follow the installation instructions on this same page on how to extract the files as some systems will not allow these to be self-extractable. A word of warning: you must use a version of the NDK above r8e with Cocos2d-x 3.x.

What just happened?

You have successfully downloaded everything you'll need to set up Cocos2d-x in your machine and start development. If you are using a Mac, you will probably need to change your security settings in **System Preferences** to allow Eclipse to run. Also, go ahead and open the Android SDK Manager inside Eclipse by going to the **Window-Android SDK Manager** menu, and install the packages for at least Version 2.3.3 and then anything above that you might wish to target.

Also, make sure you have Python installed in your machine. Inside Terminal or command prompt, just type the word `python` and hit enter. If you don't have it installed, visit `https://www.python.org/` and follow the instructions there.

So by the end of this step you should have Cocos2d-x, CocosIDE, the Android SDK the NDK, and Apache Ant all extracted inside a folder.

Now let's install Cocos2d-x.

Time for action – installing Cocos2d-x

Open Terminal or command prompt and navigate to the Cocos2d-x extracted folder:

1. You can do this by typing `cd` (that is, `cd` and a space) and then dragging the folder to the Terminal window and hitting *Enter*. In my machine this looks like:

   ```
   cd /Applications/Dev/cocos2d-x-3.4
   ```

2. Next, type `python setup.py`.

3. Hit *Enter*. You will be prompted for the paths to the NDK, SDK and Apache ANT root. You must drag each one of the folders to the Terminal window, making sure to delete any extra spaces at the end of the path and hit *Enter*. So for the NDK I get:

   ```
   /Applications/Dev/android-ndk-r10c
   ```

4. Next, it's the path for the SDK. Once again, I drag the folder that I have stored inside Eclipse's folder:

   ```
   /Applications/eclipse/sdk
   ```

5. Next, it's the path to ANT. If you have it properly installed on your machine, the path will be something like `usr/local/bin` and the setup script will find it for you. Otherwise, you can use the one you downloaded and extracted. Just point to the `bin` folder inside it:

   ```
   /Applications/Dev/apache-ant-1.9.4/bin
   ```

6. The last step is to add these paths to your system. Follow the last instruction in the window where it says: **Please execute command: "source /Users/YOUR_USER_NAME/.bash_profile" to make added system variables take effect**. You can copy the command inside the quotes, paste it, and hit *Enter*.

What just happened?

You now have Cocos2d-x installed on your machine and you're ready to go. Time to create our first project!

Hello-x World-x

Let's create that old chestnut in computer programming: the hello world example.

Time for action – creating an application

Open Terminal again and follow these easy steps:

1. You should have the path to the Cocos2d-x console already added to your system. You can test this by using the cocos command inside Terminal. In order to create a new project called HelloWorld, using C++ as its primary language and save it on your desktop, you need to run the following command, replacing YOUR_BUNDLE_INDETIFIER with a package name of your choice, and replacing PATH_TO_YOUR_PROJECT with the path to wherever you wish to save your project:

```
cocos new HelloWorld -p YOUR_BUNDLE_IDENTIFIER -l cpp -d PATH_TO_
YOUR_PROJECT
```

2. As an example, in my machine this is the line I typed:

```
cocos new HelloWorld -p com.rengelbert.HelloWorld -l cpp -d /
Users/rengelbert/Desktop/HelloWorld
```

And hit *Enter*. If you choose not to give a directory parameter (-d), the Cocos console will save the project inside the Cocos2d-x folder.

3. Now you can go to your desktop, or wherever you chose to save your project, and navigate to the folder proj.ios_mac inside the HelloWorld project. Inside that folder you'll find the Xcode project file. Once you open the project inside Xcode, you can click the **Run** button and you're done.

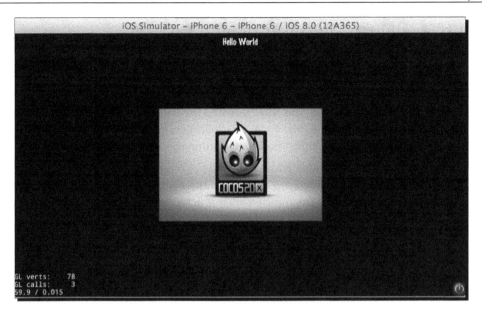

 When you run a **cocos2d-x** application in Xcode, it is quite common for the program to post some warnings regarding your code, or most likely, the frameworks. These will mostly reference deprecated methods or statements that do not precisely follow more recent and stricter rules of the current SDK. But that's okay. These warnings, though certainly annoying, can be ignored.

What just happened?

You created your first Cocos2d-x application. The parameters used on the command line are:

- ◆ -p for package or bundle identifier
- ◆ -l for language, and here, you have the option cpp, lua, or JavaScript

Now let's run this app in Android.

 Downloading the example code

You can download the example code files from your account at http://www.packtpub.com for all the Packt Publishing books you have purchased. If you purchased this book elsewhere, you can visit http://www.packtpub.com/support and register to have the files e-mailed directly to you.

Time for action – deploying to Android

We're going to open the project inside Eclipse:

1. Open Eclipse.

2. We need to fix the path to the NDK; this step may be optional in your system, and in any case, it must be done only once. Inside Eclipse, go to **Eclipse-Preferences**, then inside the **C/C++** option select **Build-Environment**.

3. You need to add the NDK path and it must be called `NDK_ROOT`. In order to do this, you must click **Add...**, and use `NDK_ROOT` as the name and then click inside the **Value** field to make sure the mouse cursor is active inside it, and then drag the NDK folder you downloaded inside the field. On my machine the result looked like this:

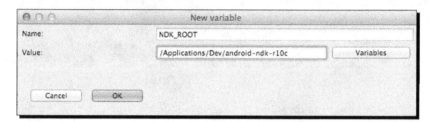

4. Click **Apply**. It might be good to restart Eclipse. (If you do not see the **C/C++** option in **Preferences,** it means you do not have the CDT plugins installed. Look for complete instructions at `http://www.eclipse.org/cdt/` on how to install them.)

5. Now we're ready to bring our project inside Eclipse. Select **File | Import...**.

6. In the dialog box, select the **Android** option, and then select the **Existing Android Code Into Workspace** option and click **Next**:

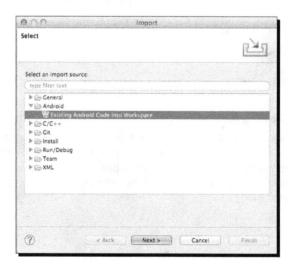

7. Click on the **Browse** button and navigate to the `HelloWorld` project, and select the `proj.android` folder inside it and hit **Next**.

8. You should see the project compiling. The entire framework library will be compiled and so will the classes used in the base template.

9. Sadly, with Version 3.4 of the framework, we have an extra step here. It was gone in Version 3.3, but now it's back. You must import the project's referenced Cocos2d-x library into Eclipse's package explorer. Repeat step 8, but instead of selecting the `proj.android` folder, select `cocos2d/cocos/platform/android/java`, and hit **Next**.

10. This will select a library called `libcocos2dx`; click on **Finish**.

11. Once that's done, it might be good to run a build just in case your project failed to generate the correct resource files. So, navigate to **Project** | **Build All**.

12. Now, connect your Android device and make sure Eclipse has recognized it. You might need to turn on **Development** options in your device, or restart your device while connected to your computer and with Eclipse running.

13. Right-click on your project folder and select **Run As** | **Android Application**.

What just happened?

You ran your first Cocos2d-x application in Android. Don't bother with the simulator for your Android builds; it's a waste of time. If you don't have a device handy, consider investing in one.

Alternatively, you could open your project's root folder inside Terminal (or command prompt) and use the Cocos2d-x console `compile` command:

```
cocos compile -p android
```

The people behind Cocos2d-x have announced they will get rid of the build Python script in the future versions of the framework, so it's good to be prepared and know how to go without it.

While working with Eclipse, you might soon be faced with the dreaded `java.lang.NullPointerException` error. This might be related to conflicts in the ADT, CDT or NDK!

 When you're faced with this error you have no option other than reinstall whatever Eclipse points to as the culprit. This might happen after an update, or if for some reason you have installed another framework that uses a path to the NDK or ADT. If the error is tied to a particular project or library, just remove all projects from the package explorer in Eclipse and reimport them.

Now let's go over the sample application and its files.

The folder structure

First you have the `Classes` folder; this will contain the classes for your application, and are written entirely in C++. Below that is the `Resources` folder, where you find the images, fonts, and any kind of media used by the application.

The `ios` folder has the necessary underlying connection between your app and iOS. For other platforms, you will have their necessary linkage files in separate folders targeting their respective platform.

It is important to maintain this file structure. So your classes will go into the `Classes` folder and all your images, sound files, fonts, level data should be placed in the `Resources` folder.

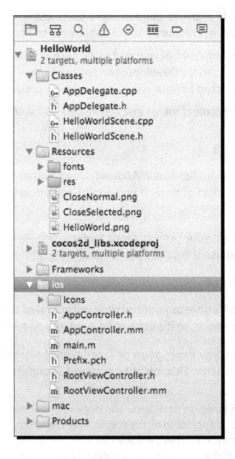

Now let's go over the main classes of the basic application.

The iOS linkage classes

`AppController` and `RootViewController` are responsible to setting up OpenGL in iOS as well as telling the underlying operating system that your application is about to say `Hello... To the World`.

These classes are written with a mix of Objective-C and C++, as all the nice brackets and the `.mm` extension show. You will change very little, if anything, on these classes; and again that will reflect in changes to the way iOS handles your application. So other targets would require the same instructions or none at all, depending on the target.

In `AppController` for instance, I could add support for multitouch. And in `RootViewController`, I could limit the screen orientations supported by my application, for instance.

The AppDelegate class

This class marks the first time your C++ app will talk to the underlying OS. It attempts to map the main events mobile devices we want to dispatch and listen to. From here on, all your application will be written in C++ (unless you need something else for a specific target) and from this point on, you can add conditional code for different targets.

In `AppDelegate`, you should set up the `Director` object (it is the Cocos2d-x all powerful singleton manager object), to run your application just the way you want. You can:

◆ Get rid of the application status information

◆ Change the frame rate of your application

◆ Tell `Director` where your high definition images are, and where your standard definition images are, as well as which to use

◆ You can change the overall scale of your application, so it will best fit different screens

◆ The `AppDelegate` class is also the best place to start any preloading process

◆ And most importantly, it is here you tell the `Director` object what `Scene` to begin your application with

Here too, you will handle what happens to your application if the OS decides to kill it, push it aside, or hang it upside down to dry. All you need to do is place your logic inside the correct event handler: `applicationDidEnterBackground` or `applicationWillEnterForeground`.

The HelloWorldScene class

When you run the application, you get a screen with the words `Hello World` and a bunch of numbers in one corner; those are the display statistics you decided you wanted around in the `AppDelegate` class.

The actual screen is created by the oddly named `HelloWorldScene` class. It is a `Layer` class that creates its own scene (don't worry if you don't know what a `Layer` or a `Scene` class is; you will know soon).

When it initializes, `HelloWorldScene` puts a button on the screen that you can press to exit the application. The button is actually a `Menu` item part of a `Menu` object that only has one button, with two image states for the button, and one call back event when the said button is pressed.

The `Menu` object automatically handles touch events targeting its members, so you don't get to see any of that code floating about. Then, there is also the necessary `Label` object to show the `Hello World` message and the background image.

Who begets whom?

If have you never worked with either Cocos2d or Cocos2d-x before, the way the initial `scene()` method is instantiated may lead to dizziness. To recap, in `AppDelegate` you have:

```
auto scene = HelloWorld::createScene();
director->runWithScene(scene);
```

`Director` needs a `Scene` object to run, which you can think of as being your application, basically. `Scene` needs something to show, and in this case, a `Layer` object will do. `Scene` is then said to contain a `Layer` object.

Here a `Scene` object is created through a static method `scene` inside a `Layer` derived class. So the layer creates the scene, and the scene immediately adds the layer to itself. Huh? Relax. This incestuous-like instantiation will most likely happen only once, and you get nothing to do with it when it happens. So you can easily ignore all these funny goings-on and look the other way. I promise instantiations will be a much easier task after this first one.

Finding more reference material

Follow these steps to access one of the best sources for reference material on Cocos2d-x: its `Test` project.

Time for action – running the test samples

You can open the test project just like you would any other Xcode/Eclipse project:

1. In Eclipse, you can import the test project from inside the Cocos2d-x folder you downloaded. You'll find it in `tests/cpp-tests/proj.android`.

2. You can follow the same steps as before to build this project.

3. In Xcode, you must open the tests project file that you'll find in the Cocos2d-x framework folder inside the `build` folder: `build/cocos2d_tests.xcodeproj`.

4. Once the project is opened in Xcode, you must select the correct target next to the **Run** button as follows:

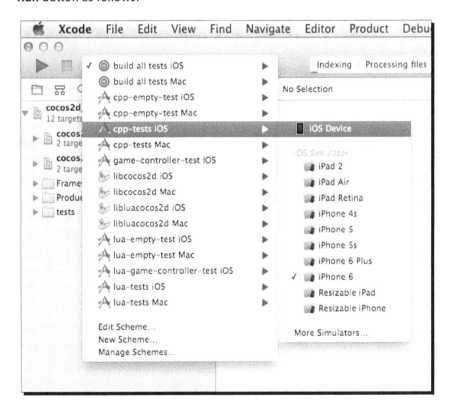

5. In order to actually review the code inside the tests, you may navigate to `tests/cpp-tests/Classes` for the C++ tests or `tests/lua-tests/src` for the Lua tests. Better yet, if you have a program such as `TextWrangler` or an equivalent, you can open these entire directories inside a **Disk Browser** window and have all that information ready for referencing right at your desktop.

What just happened?

With the test samples, you can visualize most features in Cocos2d-x, what they do, as well as see some of the ways you can initialize and customize them.

I will refer to the code found in the tests quite often. As usual with programming, there is always a different way to accomplish the same task, so sometimes, after showing you one way, I'll refer to a different one that you can find (and by then easily understand) inside the `Test` classes.

The other tools

Now comes the part where you may need to spend a bit more money to get some extremely helpful tools (and do some extra bit of learning). In this book's examples, I use four of them:

♦   A tool to help build sprite sheets: I'll use **TexturePacker** (`http://www.codeandweb.com/texturepacker`). There are other alternatives, such as **Zwoptex** (`http://zwopple.com/zwoptex/`), and they usually offer some features for free. Cocos2d-x now offers a free program called **CocosStudio**, which is somewhat similar to **SpriteBuilder** (previously **CocosBuilder**), and it offers ways to build sprite sheets, bitmap fonts, as well as a number of other goodies. At the time of writing this, the Windows version is somewhat superior to the Mac version, but they are free!

♦   A tool to help build particle effects: I'll use Particle Designer (`http://www.71squared.com/en/particledesigner`). Depending on your operating system, you may find free tools online for this. Cocos2d-x comes bundled with some common particle effects that you can customize. But doing it blindly is a process I do not recommend. CocosStudio also allows you to create your own particle effects, but you may find its interface a bit daunting. It certainly requires its own book of tutorials!

♦   A tool to help build bitmap fonts: I'll use Glyph Designer (`http://www.71squared.com/en/glyphdesigner`). But there are others: bmGlyph (which is not as expensive) and FontBuilder (which is free). It is not extremely hard to build a bitmap font—not nearly as hard as building a particle effect from scratch—but doing it once is enough to convince you to get one of these tools fast. Once again, you might give CocosStudio a go.

♦   A tool to produce sound effects: No contest—sfxr for Windows or its Mac port cfxr. Both are free (`http://www.drpetter.se/project_sfxr.html` and `http://thirdcog.eu/apps/cfxr`, respectively).

Summary

You just learned how to install Cocos2d-x and create a basic application. You also learned enough of the structure of a basic Cocos2d-x application to start building your first game and you know how to deploy to both iOS and Android.

Keep the `Test` classes by your side as you go over the examples in this book and you will be a Cocos2d-x pro in no time!

But first, let's go over a few things regarding the framework and its native language.

2

You Plus C++ Plus Cocos2d-x

This chapter will be aimed at two types of developers: the original Cocos2d developer who is scared of C++ but won't admit it to his friends and the C++ coder who never even heard of Cocos2d and finds Objective-C funny looking.

I'll go over the main syntax differences Objective-C developers should pay attention to and the few code style changes involved in developing with Cocos2d-x that C++ developers should be aware of. But first, a quick introduction to Cocos2d-x and what it is all about.

You will learn the following topics:

◆ What Cocos2d-x is and what it can do for you

◆ How to create classes in C++

◆ How to memory manage your objects in Cocos2d-x and C++

◆ What you get out of Ref

Cocos2d-x – an introduction

So what is a 2D framework? If I had to define it in as few words as possible, I'd say rectangles in a loop.

At the heart of Cocos2d-x, you find the `Sprite` class and what that class does, in simple terms, is keep a reference to two very important rectangles. One is the image (or texture) rectangle, also called the source rectangle, and the other is the destination rectangle. If you want an image to appear in the center of the screen, you will use `Sprite`. You will pass it the information of what and where that image source is and where on the screen you want it to appear.

There is not much that needs to be done to the first rectangle, the source one; but there is a lot that can be changed in the destination rectangle, including its position on the screen, its size, opacity, rotation, and so on.

Cocos2d-x will then take care of all the OpenGL drawing necessary to display your image where you want it and how you want it, and it will do so inside a render loop. Your code will most likely tap into that same loop to update its own logic.

Pretty much any 2D game you can think of can be built with Cocos2d-x with a few sprites and a loop.

 In Version 3.x of the framework, there was a mild separation between Cocos2d-x and its counterpart Cocos2d. It dropped the prefix CC in favor of namespaces, embraced C++11 features, and became that much nicer to work with because of it.

Containers

Also important in Cocos2d-x is the notion of containers (or nodes). These are all the objects that can have sprites inside them (or other nodes.) This is extremely useful at times because by changing aspects of the container, you automatically change aspects of its children. Move the container and all its children will move with it. Rotate the container and well, you get the picture!

The containers are: Scene, Layer, and Sprite. They all inherit from a base container class called **node**. Each container will have its peculiarities, but basically you will arrange them as follows:

- Scene: This will contain one or more Node, usually Layer types. It is common to break applications into multiple scenes; for instance, one for the main menu, one for settings, and one for the actual game. Technically, each scene will behave as a separate entity in your application, almost as subapplications themselves, and you can run a series of transition effects when changing between scenes.

- Layer: This will most likely contain Sprite. There are a number of specialized Layer objects aimed at saving you, the developer, some time in creating things such as menus for instance (Menu), or a colored background (LayerColor). You can have more than one Layer per scene, but good planning makes this usually unnecessary.

- ◆ `Sprite`: This will contain your images and be added as children to `Layer` derived containers. To my mind, this is the most important class in all of Cocos2d-x, so much so, that after your application initializes, when both a `Scene` and a `Layer` object are created, you could build your entire game only with sprites and never use another container class in Cocos2d-x.

- ◆ `Node`: This super class to all containers blurs the line between itself and `Layer`, and even `Sprite` at times. It has its own set of specialized subclasses (besides the ones mentioned earlier), such as `MotionStreak`, `ParallaxNode`, and `SpriteBatchNode`, to name a few. It can, with a few adjustments, behave just as `Layer`. But most of the time you will use it to create your own specialized nodes or as a general reference in polymorphism.

The Director and cache classes

After containers comes the all-knowing `Director` and all-encompassing cache objects. The `Director` object manages scenes and knows all about your application. You will make calls to it to get to that information and to change some of the things such as screen size, frame rate, scale factor, and so forth.

The caches are collector objects. The most important ones are `TextureCache`, `SpriteFrameCache`, and `AnimationCache`. These are responsible for storing key information regarding those two important rectangles I mentioned about earlier. But every type of data that is used repeatedly in Cocos2d-x will be kept in some sort of cache list.

Both `Director` and all cache objects are singletons. These are special sort of classes that are instantiated only once; and this one instance can be accessed by any other object.

The other stuff

After the basic containers, the caches and the `Director` object, comes the remaining 90 percent of the framework. Among all this, you will find:

- ◆ **Actions**: Animations will be handled through these and what a treat they are!

- ◆ **Particles**: Particles systems for your delight.

- ◆ **Specialized nodes**: For things such as menus, progress bars, special effects, parallax effect, tile maps, and much, much more.

- ◆ **The macros, structures, and helper methods**: Hundreds of time-saving, magical bits of logic. You don't need to know them all, but chances are that you will be coding something that can be easily replaced by a macro or a helper method and feel incredibly silly when you find out about it later.

Do you know C++?

Don't worry, the C part is easy. The first plus goes by really fast, but that second plus, oh boy!

Remember, it is C. And if you have coded in Objective-C with the original Cocos2d, you know good old C already even if you saw it in between brackets most of the time.

But C++ also has classes, just like Objective-C, and these classes are declared in the interface files just like in Objective-C. So let's go over the creation of a C++ class.

The class interface

This will be done in a `.h` file. We'll use a text editor to create this file since I don't want any code hinting and autocompletion features getting in the way of you learning the basics of C++ syntax. So for now at least, open up your favorite text editor. Let's create a class interface!

Time for action – creating the interface

The interface, or header file, is just a text file with the `.h` extension.

1. Create a new text file and save it as `HelloWorld.h`. Then, enter the following lines at the top:

```
#ifndef __HELLOWORLD_H__
#define __HELLOWORLD_H__
#include "cocos2d.h"
```

2. Next, add the namespace declaration:

```
using namespace cocos2d;
```

3. Then, declare your class name and the name of any inherited classes:

```
class HelloWorld : public cocos2d::Layer {
```

4. Next, we add the properties and methods:

```
protected:
int _score;

public:

    HelloWorld();
    virtual ~HelloWorld();

    virtual bool init();
    static cocos2d::Scene* scene();
    CREATE_FUNC(HelloWorld);
    void update(float dt);
    inline int addTwoIntegers (int one, int two) {
```

```
            return one + two;
    }
};
```

5. We finish by closing the #ifndef statement:

```
#endif // __HELLOWORLD_H__
```

What just happened?

You created a header file in C++. Let's go over the important bits of information:

◆ In C++ you include, you do not import. The import statement in Objective-C checks whether something needs to be included; include does not. But we accomplish the same thing through that clever use of definitions at the top. There are other ways to run the same check (with #pragma once, for instance) but this one is added to any new C++ files you create in Xcode.

◆ You can make your life easier by declaring the namespaces you'll use in the class. These are similar to packages in some languages. You may have noticed that all the uses of cocos2d:: in the code are not necessary because of the namespace declaration. But I wanted to show you the bit you can get rid of by adding a namespace declaration.

◆ So next you give your class a name and you may choose to inherit from some other class. In C++ you can have as many super classes as you want. And you must declare whether your super class is public or not.

◆ You declare your public, protected and private methods and members between the curly braces. HelloWorld is the constructor and ~HelloWorld is the destructor (it will do what dealloc does in Objective-C).

◆ The virtual keyword is related to overrides. When you mark a method as virtual, you are telling the compiler not to set in stone the owner of the method, but to keep it in memory as execution will reveal the obvious owner. Otherwise, the compiler may erroneously decide that a method belongs to the super and not its inheriting class.

Also, it's good practice to make all your destructors virtual. You only need use the keyword once in the super class to mark potential overrides, but it is common practice to repeat the virtual keyword in all subclasses so developers know which methods are overrides (C++11 adds a tag override, which makes this distinction even clearer, and you will see examples of it in this book's code). In this case, init comes from Layer and HelloWorld wants to override it.

```
virtual bool init();
```

◆ Oh yes, in C++ you must declare overrides in your interfaces. No exceptions!

The `inline` method is something new to you, probably. These methods are added to the code by the compiler wherever they are called for. So every time I make a call to `addTwoIntegers`, the compiler will replace it with the lines for the method declared in the interface. So the `inline` method works just as statements inside a method; they do not require their own bit of memory in the stack. But if you have a two-line `inline` method called 50 times in your program, it means that the compiler will add a hundred lines to your code.

The class implementation

This will be done in a `.cpp` file. So let's go back to our text editor and create the implementation for our `HelloWorld` class.

Time for action – creating the implementation

The implementation is a text file with the `.cpp` extension:

1. Create a new text file and save it as `HelloWorld.cpp`. At the top, let's start by including our header file:

    ```
    #include "HelloWorld.h"
    ```

2. Next, we implement our constructor and destructor:

    ```
    HelloWorld::HelloWorld () {
        //constructor
    }

    HelloWorld::~HelloWorld () {
        //destructor
    }
    ```

3. Then comes our static method:

    ```
    Scene* HelloWorld::scene() {
        auto scene = Scene::create();

        auto layer = HelloWorld::create();

        scene->addChild(layer);

        return scene;
    }
    ```

4. And then come our two remaining public methods:

```
bool HelloWorld::init() {
    // call to super
    if ( !Layer::init() )
    {
        return false;
    }

    //create main loop
    this->scheduleUpdate();

    return true;
}

void HelloWorld::update (float dt) {
    //the main loop
}
```

What just happened?

We created the implementation for our `HelloWorld` class. Here are the most important bits to take notice of:

- The `HelloWorld::` scope resolution is not optional here. Every single method declared in your interface belongs to the new class that needs the correct scope resolution in the implementation file.

- You also need the scope resolution when calling the super class like `Layer::init()`. There is no built-in `super` keyword in the standard C++ library.

- You use `this` instead of `self`. The `->` notation is used when you're trying to access an object's properties or methods through a pointer to the object (a pointer is the information of where you find the actual object in memory). The `.` (dot) notation is used to access an object's methods and properties through its actual instance (the blob of memory that comprises the actual object).

- We create an `update` loop, which takes a float for its delta time value simply by calling `scheduleUpdate`. You will see more options related to this later in this book.

- You can use the `auto` keyword as the type of an object if it's obvious enough to the compiler which type an object is.

- The `inline` methods, of course, are not implemented in the class since they exist only in the interface.

And that's enough of syntax for now. C++ is one of the most extensive languages out there and I do not wish to leave you with the impression that I have covered all of it. But it is a language made by developers for developers. Trust me, you will feel right at home working with it.

The information listed previously will become clearer once we move on to building the games. But now, onwards to the big scary monster: memory management.

Instantiating objects and managing memory

There is no **Automatic Reference Counting (ARC)** in Cocos2d-x, so Objective-C developers who have forgotten memory management might have a problem here. However, the rule regarding memory management is very simple with C++: if you use `new`, you must delete. C++11 makes this even easier by introducing special pointers that are memory-managed (these are `std::unique_ptr` and `std::shared_ptr`).

Cocos2d-x, however, will add a few other options and commands to help with memory management, similar to the ones we have in Objective-C (without ARC). This is because Cocos2d-x, unlike C++ and very much like Objective-C, has a root class. The framework is more than just a C++ port of Cocos2d. It also ports certain notions of Objective-C to C++ in order to recreate its memory-management system.

Cocos2d-x has a `Ref` class that is the root of every major object in the framework. It allows the framework to have `autorelease` pools and `retain` counts, as well other Objective-C equivalents.

When instantiating Cocos2d-x objects, you have basically two options:

♦ Using static methods
♦ The C++ and Cocos2d-x style

Using static methods

Using static methods is the recommended way. The three-stage instantiation process of Objective-C, with `alloc`, `init`, and `autorelease/retain`, is recreated here. So, for instance, a `Player` class, which extends `Sprite`, might have the following methods:

```
Player::Player () {
    this->setPosition  ( Vec2(0,0) );
}

Player* Player::create () {

    auto player = new Player();
```

```
    if (player && player->initWithSpriteFrameName("player.png")) {
        player->autorelease();
        return player;
    }
    CC_SAFE_DELETE(player);
    return nullptr;
}
```

For instantiation, you call the static `create` method. It will create a new `Player` object as an empty husk version of `Player`. No major initialization should happen inside the constructor, just in case you may have to delete the object due to some failure in the instantiation process. Cocos2d-x has a series of macros for object deletion and release, like the `CC_SAFE_DELETE` macro used previously.

You then initialize the super through one of its available methods. In Cocos2d-x, these `init` methods return a `boolean` value for success. You may now begin filling the `Player` object with some data.

If successful, then initialize your object with its proper data if not done in the previous step, and return it as an `autorelease` object.

So in your code the object would be instantiated as follows:

```
auto player = Player::create();
this->addChild(player);//this will retain the object
```

Even if the `player` variable were a member of the class (say, `m_player`), you wouldn't have to retain it to keep it in scope. By adding the object to some Cocos2d-x list or cache, the object is automatically retained. So you may continue to address that memory through its pointer:

```
m_player = Player::create();
this->addChild(m_player);//this will retain the object
//m_player still references the memory address
//but does not need to be released or deleted by you
```

The C++ and Cocos2d-x style

In this option, you would instantiate the previous `Player` object as follows:

```
auto player = new Player();
player->initWithSpriteFrameName("player.png");
this->addChild(player);
player->autorelease();
```

`Player` could do without a static method in this case and the `player` pointer will not access the same memory in future as it's set to be autoreleased (so it would not stick around for long). In this case, however, the memory would not leak. It would still be retained by a Cocos2d-x list (the `addChild` command takes care of that). You can still access that memory by going over the children list added to `this`.

If you needed the pointer to be a member property you could use `retain()` instead of `autorelease()`:

```
m_player = new Player();
m_player->initWithSpriteFrameName("player.png");
this->addChild(m_player);
m_player->retain();
```

Then sometime later, you would have to release it; otherwise, it will leak:

```
m_player->release();
```

Hardcore C++ developers may choose to forget all about the `autorelease` pool and simply use `new` and `delete`:

```
Player * player = new Player();
player->initWithSpriteFrameName("player.png");
this->addChild(player);
delete player;//This will crash!
```

This will not work. You have to use `autorelease`, `retain`, or leave the previous code without the `delete` command and hope there won't be any leak.

C++ developers must keep in mind that `Ref` is managed by the framework. This means that objects are being internally added to caches and the `autorelease` pool even though you may not want this to happen. When you create that `Player` sprite, for instance, the `player.png` file you used will be added to the texture cache, or the sprite frame cache. When you add the sprite to a layer, the sprite will be added to a list of all children of that layer, and this list will be managed by the framework. My advice is, relax and let the framework work for you.

Non-C++ developers should keep in mind that any class not derived from `Ref` should be managed the usual way, that is, if *you* are creating a new object you must delete it at some point:

```
MyObject* object = new MyObject();
delete object;
```

What you get with Ref

With `Ref` you get managed objects. This means that `Ref` derived objects will have a reference count property, which will be used to determine whether an object should be deleted from memory or not. The reference count is updated every time an object is added or removed from a Cocos2d-x collection object.

For instance, Cocos2d-x comes with a `Vector` collection object that extends the functionality of the C++ standard library vector (`std::vector`) by increasing and decreasing the reference count when objects are added and removed from it. For that reason, it can only store `Ref` derived objects.

Once again, every `Ref` derived class can be managed the way things used to be managed in Objective-C before ARC- with `retain` counts and `autorelease` pools.

C++, however, comes packed with its own wonderful dynamic list classes, similar to the ones you would find in Java and C#. But for `Ref` derived objects, you would probably be best served by Cocos2d-x managed lists, or else remember to retain and release each object when applicable. If you create a class which does not extend `Ref` and you need to store instances of this class in a list container, then choose the standard library ones.

In the examples that follow in this book I will code primarily from within the framework, so you will get to see plenty of examples of `cocos2d::Vector` being used, for instance, but I will also use a `std::vector` instance or two in some of the games.

Summary

Hopefully, non-C++ developers have now learned that there is nothing to be feared from the language, and hardcore C++ developers have not scoffed too much at the notion of a root class and its retains and autoreleases.

All the stuff that root classes have brought to languages such as Java and Objective-C will forever be a moot point. The creepy, underlying operations that go on behind your back with root objects cannot be shut down or controlled. They are not optional, and this forceful nature of root objects has bothered C++ developers ever since notions such as garbage collectors first surfaced.

Having said that, memory management of `Ref` objects is extremely helpful and I hope even the most distrustful developers will soon learn to be thankful for it.

Furthermore, Cocos2d-x is awesome. So let's create a game already!

3
Your First Game – Air Hockey

We are going to build an Air Hockey game to introduce you to all the main aspects of building a project with Cocos2d-x. These include setting up the project's configuration, loading images, loading sounds, building a game for more than one screen resolution, and managing touch events.

Oh, and you will need to call a friend. This is a two player game. Go on, I'll wait here.

By the end of this chapter, you will know:

◆ How to build an iPad-only game

◆ How to enable multitouch

◆ How to support both retina and non-retina displays

◆ How to load images and sounds

◆ How to play sound effects

◆ How to create sprites

◆ How to extend the Cocos2d-x `Sprite` class

◆ How to create labels and update them

Without further ado...let's begin.

Game configurations

The game will have the following characteristics:

◆ It must support multitouch since it's a two player game

◆ It must be played on large screens since it's a two player game

◆ It must support retina displays because we want to cash in on that

◆ It must be played only in portrait mode because I built the art in portrait

So let's create our project!

Time for action – creating your game project

I'll build the game first in Xcode and then show how to take the project to Eclipse, but the folder structure remains the same, so you can work with any IDE you wish and the instructions here will be the same:

1. Open the terminal and create a new Cocos2d-x project called `AirHockey` that uses C++ as its main language. I saved mine on the desktop, so the command I had to enter looks like this:

```
cocos new AirHockey -p com.rengelbert.AirHockey -l cpp -d /Users/
rengelbert/Desktop/AirHockey
```

2. Once the project is created, navigate to its `proj.ios_mac` folder and double-click on the `AirHockey.xcodeproj` file. (For Eclipse, you can follow the same steps we did when we created the `HelloWorld` project to import the project.)

3. Select the top item in **Project Navigator** and making sure the **iOS** target is selected, edit the information by navigating to **General | Deployment info**, setting the target device to **iPad** and **Device Orientation** to **Portrait** and **Upside Down**.

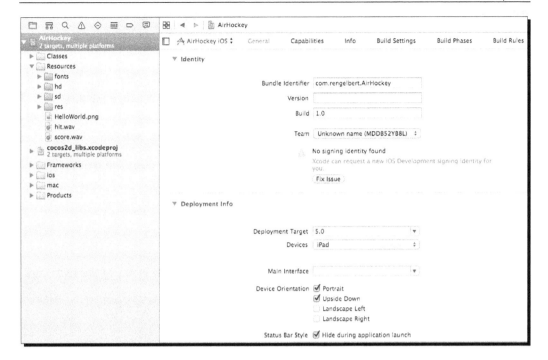

4. Save your project changes.

What just happened?

You created a Cocos2d-x project targeting iPads, and you are ready to set it up with the rest of the configurations I described earlier.

So let's do that now.

Time for action – laying down the rules

We'll update the `RootViewController.mm` file.

1. Go to `RootViewController.mm` inside the `ios` folder and look for the `shouldAutorotateToInterfaceOrientation` method. Change the line inside the method to read:

```
return UIInterfaceOrientationIsPortrait( interfaceOrientation );
```

2. And a few lines below in the `supportedInterfaceOrientations` method, change the line inside the conditional to:

```
return UIInterfaceOrientationMaskPortrait;
```

What just happened?

We just told `RootViewController` we want our application to play in any of the two supported portrait modes.

Supporting retina displays

Now let's add the images to our project.

Time for action – adding the image files

First, we download the resources for this project, and then we add them in Xcode.

1. Go to this book's **Support** page (`www.packtpub.com/support`) and download the `4198_03_RESOURCES.zip` file. Inside it, you should find three folders called `hd`, `sd`, and `fonts`.

2. Go to your `Project` folder, the actual folder in your system. Drag the three folders to the `Resources` folder inside your project.

3. Go back to Xcode. Select the `Resources` folder in your project navigation panel. Then go to **File | Add Files to AirHockey**.

4. In the **File** window, navigate to the `Resources` folder and select the `sd`, `hd`, and `fonts` folders.

5. This is very important: make sure **Create folder references for any added folders** is selected. Also make sure you selected **AirHockey** as the target. It wouldn't hurt to make sure **Copy items to destination...** is also selected.

6. Click on **Add**.

What just happened?

You added the necessary image files for your Air Hockey game. These come in two versions: one for retina displays (high definition) and one for non-retina displays (standard definition). It is very important that references are added to the actual folders, only this way Xcode will be able to have two files with the same name inside the project and still keep them apart; one in each folder. We also added the font we'll be using in the game.

Now let's tell Cocos2d-x where to look for the correct files.

Time for action – adding retina support

This time we'll work with the class `AppDelegate.cpp`:

1. Go to `AppDelegate.cpp` (you'll find it in the `Classes` folder). Inside the `applicationDidFinishLaunching` method, and below the `director->setAnimationInterval(1.0 / 60)` line, add the following lines:

```
auto screenSize = glview->getFrameSize();
auto designSize = Size(768, 1024);
glview->setDesignResolutionSize(designSize.width, designSize.
height, ResolutionPolicy::EXACT_FIT);

std::vector<std::string> searchPaths;
if (screenSize.width > 768) {
    searchPaths.push_back("hd");
    director->setContentScaleFactor(2);
} else {
    searchPaths.push_back("sd");
    director->setContentScaleFactor(1);
}
auto fileUtils = FileUtils::getInstance();
fileUtils->setSearchPaths(searchPaths);
```

2. Save the file.

What just happened?

An entire book could be written about this topic, although in this first example, we have a very simple implementation on how to support multiple screen sizes since we are only targeting iPads. Here we are saying: "Hey `AppDelegate`, I designed this game for a 768 x 1024 screen."

All the values for positioning and font size were chosen for that screen size. If the screen is larger, make sure you grab the files from the hd folder and change the scale by which you will multiply all my positioning and font sizes. If the screen has the same size I designed the game for, use the files in the sd folder and set the scale to 1. (Android adds even more complexity to this, but we'll tackle that in later in the book.)

`FileUtils` will look for every file you load for your game first inside Resources | sd (or hd). If it doesn't find them there, it will try to find them in Resources. This is a good thing because files shared by both versions may be added only once to the project, inside Resources. That is what we'll do now with the sound files.

Adding sound effects

This game has two files for sound effects. You will find them in the same .zip file you downloaded previously.

Time for action – adding the sound files

Assuming you have the sound files from the downloaded resources, let's add them to the project.

1. Drag both the .wav files to the Resources folder inside your Project folder.

2. Then go to Xcode, select the Resources folder in the file navigation panel and select **File | Add Files to AirHockey**.

3. Make sure the **AirHockey** target is selected.

4. Go to AppDelegate.cpp again. At the top, add this include statement:

   ```
   #include "SimpleAudioEngine.h"
   ```

5. Then below the USING_NS_CC macro (for using namespace cocos2d), add:

   ```
   using namespace CocosDenshion;
   ```

6. Then just below the lines you added in the previous section, inside applicationDidFinishLaunching, add the following lines:

   ```
   auto audioEngine = SimpleAudioEngine::getInstance();
   audioEngine->preloadEffect( fileUtils->fullPathForFilename("hit.
   wav").c_str() );
   audioEngine->preloadEffect( fileUtils->fullPathForFilename("score.
   wav").c_str() );
   audioEngine->setBackgroundMusicVolume(0.5f);
   audioEngine->setEffectsVolume(0.5f);
   ```

What just happened?

With the `preloadEffect` method from `CocosDenshion`, you manage to preload the files as well as instantiate and initialize `SimpleAudioEngine`. This step will always take a toll on your application's processing power, so it's best to do it early on.

By now, the folder structure for your game should look like this:

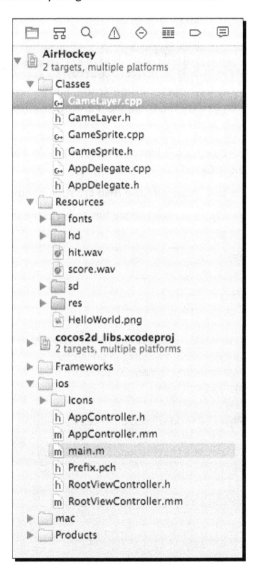

Extending Sprite

No, there is nothing wrong with Sprite. I just picked a game where we need a bit more information from some of its sprites. In this case, we want to store where a sprite is and where it will be once the current iteration of the game is completed. We will also need a helper method to get the sprite's radius.

So let's create our GameSprite class.

Time for action – adding GameSprite.cpp

From here on, we'll create any new classes inside Xcode, but you could do it just as easily in Eclipse if you remember to update the Make file. I'll show you how to do that later in this chapter.

1. In Xcode, select the Classes folder and then go to **File** | **New** | **File** and navigate to **iOS** | **Source** select **C++ File**.

2. Call it GameSprite and make sure the **Also create a header file** option is selected.

3. Select the new GameSprite.h interface file and replace the code there with this:

```
#ifndef __GAMESPRITE_H__
#define __GAMESPRITE_H__
#include "cocos2d.h"
using namespace cocos2d;
class GameSprite : public Sprite {
public:
    CC_SYNTHESIZE(Vec2, _nextPosition, NextPosition);
    CC_SYNTHESIZE(Vec2, _vector, Vector);
    CC_SYNTHESIZE(Touch*, _touch, Touch);
    GameSprite();
    virtual ~GameSprite();
    static GameSprite* gameSpriteWithFile(const char*
pszFileName);
    virtual void setPosition(const Vec2& pos) override;
    float radius();
};
#endif // __GAMESPRITE_H__
```

What just happened?

In the interface, we declare the class to be a subclass of the public `Sprite` class.

Then we add three synthesized properties. In Cocos2d-x, these are macros to create getters and setters. You declare the type, the protected variable name, and the words that will be appended to the `get` and `set` methods. So in the first `CC_SYNTHESIZE` method, the `getNextPosition` and `setNextPosition` method will be created to deal with the `Point` value inside the `_nextPosition` protected variable.

We also add the constructor and destructor for our class, and the ubiquitous static method for instantiation. This receives as a parameter, the image filename used by the sprite. We finish off by overriding `setPosition` from `Sprite` and adding the declaration for our helper method radius.

The next step then is to implement our new class.

Time for action – implementing GameSprite

With the header out of the way, all we need to do is implement our methods.

1. Select the `GameSprite.cpp` file and let's start on the instantiation logic of the class:

```
#include "GameSprite.h"

GameSprite::GameSprite(void){
    _vector = Vec2(0,0);
}

GameSprite::~GameSprite(void){
}

GameSprite* GameSprite::gameSpriteWithFile(const char *
pszFileName) {
    auto sprite = new GameSprite();
    if (sprite && sprite->initWithFile(pszFileName)) {
            sprite->autorelease();
            return sprite;
    }
    CC_SAFE_DELETE(sprite);
    return sprite = nullptr;
}
```

2. Next we need to override the `Node` method `setPosition`. We need to make sure that whenever we change the position of the sprite, the new value is also used by `_nextPosition`:

```
void GameSprite::setPosition(const Point& pos) {
    Sprite::setPosition(pos);
    if (!_nextPosition.equals(pos)) {
        _nextPosition = pos;
    }
}
```

3. And finally, we implement our new method to retrieve the radius of our sprite, which we determine to be half its texture's width:

```
float GameSprite::radius() {
    return getTexture()->getContentSize().width * 0.5f;
}
```

What just happened?

Things only begin happening in the static method. We create a new `GameSprite` class, then we call `initWithFile` on it. This is a `GameSprite` method inherited from its super class; it returns a Boolean value for whether that operation succeeded. The static method ends by returning an `autorelease` version of the `GameSprite` object.

The `setPosition` override makes sure `_nextPosition` receives the position information whenever the sprite is placed somewhere. And the helper `radius` method returns half of the sprite's texture width.

Have a go hero

Change the radius method to an inline method in the interface and remove it from the implementation file.

The actual game scene

Finally, we'll get to see all our work and have some fun with it. But first, let's delete the `HelloWorldScene` class (both header and implementation files). You'll get a few errors in the project so let's fix these.

References to the class must be changed at two lines in `AppDelegate.cpp`. Go ahead and change the references to a `GameLayer` class.

We'll create that class next.

Time for action – coding the GameLayer interface

`GameLayer` is the main container in our game.

1. Follow the steps to add a new file to your `Classes` folder. This is a C++ file called `GameLayer`.

2. Select your `GameLayer.h`. Just below the first `define` preprocessor command, add:

    ```
    #define GOAL_WIDTH 400
    ```

3. We define the width of the goals in pixels.

4. Next, add the declarations for our sprites and our score text labels:

    ```
    #include "cocos2d.h"
    #include "GameSprite.h"

    using namespace cocos2d;

    class GameLayer : public Layer
    {
        GameSprite* _player1;
        GameSprite* _player2;
        GameSprite* _ball;

        Vector<GameSprite*> _players;
        Label* _player1ScoreLabel;
        Label* _player2ScoreLabel;
    ```

    We have the `GameSprite` objects for two players (the weird looking things called mallets), and the ball (called a puck). We'll store the two players in a Cocos2d-x `Vector`. We also have two text labels to display the score for each player.

5. Declare a variable to store the screen size. We'll use this a lot for positioning:

    ```
    Size _screenSize;
    ```

6. Add variables to store the score information and a method to update these scores on screen:

    ```
    int _player1Score;
    int _player2Score;

    void playerScore (int player);
    ```

7. Finally, let's add our methods:

```
public:

    GameLayer();
    virtual ~GameLayer();
    virtual bool init();

    static Scene* scene();

    CREATE_FUNC(GameLayer);

    void onTouchesBegan(const std::vector<Touch*> &touches,
Event* event);
    void onTouchesMoved(const std::vector<Touch*> &touches,
Event* event);
    void onTouchesEnded(const std::vector<Touch*> &touches,
Event* event);

    void update (float dt);
};
#endif // __GAMELAYER_H__
```

There are constructor and destructor methods, then the `Layer init` methods, and finally the event handlers for the touch events and our loop method called `update`. These touch event handlers will be added to our class to handle when users' touches begin, when they move across the screen, and when they end.

What just happened?

`GameLayer` is our game. It contains references to all the sprites we need to control and update, as well as all game data.

In the class implementation, all the logic starts inside the `init` method.

Time for action – implementing init()

Inside `init()`, we'll build the game screen, bringing in all the sprites and labels we'll need for the game:

1. So right after the `if` statement where we call the super `Layer::init` method, we add:

```
_players = Vector<GameSprite*>(2);
_player1Score = 0;
_player2Score = 0;
_screenSize = Director::getInstance()->getWinSize();
```

2. We create the vector where we'll store both players, initialize the score values, and grab the screen size from the singleton, all-knowing `Director`. We'll use the screen size to position all sprites relatively. Next we will create our first sprite. It is created with an image filename, which `FileUtils` will take care of loading from the correct folder:

```
auto court = Sprite::create("court.png");
court->setPosition(Vec2(_screenSize.width * 0.5, _screenSize.
height * 0.5));
this->addChild(court);
```

3. Get into the habit of positioning sprites with relative values, and not absolute ones, so we can support more screen sizes. And say hello to the `Vec2` type definition used to create points; you'll be seeing it a lot in Cocos2d-x.

4. We finish by adding the sprite as a child to our `GameLayer` (the court sprite does not need to be a `GameSprite`).

5. Next we will use our spanking new `GameSprite` class, carefully positioning the objects on screen:

```
_player1 = GameSprite::gameSpriteWithFile("mallet.png");
_player1->setPosition(Vec2(_screenSize.width * 0.5,
_player1->radius() * 2));
_players.pushBack(_player1);
this->addChild(_player1);

_player2 = GameSprite::gameSpriteWithFile("mallet.png");
_player2->setPosition(Vec2(_screenSize.width * 0.5, _screenSize.
height - _player1->radius() * 2));
_players.pushBack(_player2);
this->addChild(_player2);
_ball = GameSprite::gameSpriteWithFile("puck.png");
_ball->setPosition(Vec2(_screenSize.width * 0.5, _screenSize.
height * 0.5 - 2 * _ball->radius()));
this->addChild(_ball);
```

6. We will create TTF labels with the `Label` class `createWithTTF` static method, passing as parameters the initial string value (0), and the path to the font file. We will then position and rotate the labels:

```
_player1ScoreLabel = Label::createWithTTF("0",
"fonts/Arial.ttf", 60);
_player1ScoreLabel->setPosition(Vec2(_screenSize.width - 60,
_screenSize.height * 0.5 - 80));
_player1ScoreLabel->setRotation(90);
this->addChild(_player1ScoreLabel);
```

```
_player2ScoreLabel = Label::createWithTTF("0",
"fonts/Arial.ttf", 60);
_player2ScoreLabel->setPosition(Vec2(_screenSize.width - 60,
_screenSize.height * 0.5 + 80));
_player2ScoreLabel->setRotation(90);
this->addChild(_player2ScoreLabel);
```

7. Then we turn `GameLayer` into a multitouch event listener and tell the `Director` event dispatcher that `GameLayer` wishes to listen to those events. And we finish by scheduling the game's main loop as follows:

```
auto listener = EventListenerTouchAllAtOnce::create();
listener->onTouchesBegan =
CC_CALLBACK_2(GameLayer::onTouchesBegan, this);
listener->onTouchesMoved =
CC_CALLBACK_2(GameLayer::onTouchesMoved, this);
listener->onTouchesEnded =
CC_CALLBACK_2(GameLayer::onTouchesEnded, this);
_eventDispatcher->addEventListenerWithSceneGraphPriority(listener,
this);
//create main loop
this->scheduleUpdate();
return true;
```

What just happened?

You created the game screen for Air Hockey, with your own sprites and labels. The game screen, once all elements are added, should look like this:

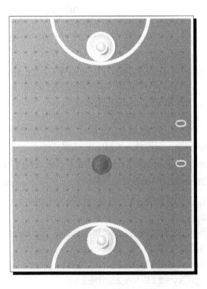

And now we're ready to handle the player's screen touches.

Time for action – handling multitouches

There are three methods we need to implement in this game to handle touches.
Each method receives, as one of its parameters, a vector of Touch objects:

1. So add our onTouchesBegan method:

```
void GameLayer::onTouchesBegan(const std::vector<Touch*> &touches,
Event* event)
{
   for( auto touch : touches) {
     if(touch != nullptr) {
        auto tap = touch->getLocation();
        for (auto player : _players) {
         if (player->boundingBox().containsPoint(tap)) {
            player->setTouch(touch);
         }
        }
     }
   }
}
```

Each GameSprite, if you recall, has a _touch property.

So we iterate through the touches, grab their location on screen, loop through
the players in the vector, and determine if the touch lands on one of the players.
If so, we store the touch inside the player's _touch property (from the
GameSprite class).

A similar process is repeated for onTouchesMoved and onTouchesEnded, so you
can copy and paste the code and just replace what goes on inside the _players
array for loop.

2. In TouchesMoved, when we loop through the players, we do this:

```
for (auto player : _players) {
  if (player->getTouch() != nullptr && player->getTouch() ==
touch) {
     Point nextPosition = tap;
   if (nextPosition.x < player->radius())
      nextPosition.x = player->radius();
   if (nextPosition.x > _screenSize.width - player->radius())
      nextPosition.x = _screenSize.width - player->radius();
   if (nextPosition.y < player->radius())
```

```
        nextPosition.y  = player->radius();
     if (nextPosition.y > _screenSize.height - player->radius())
        nextPosition.y = _screenSize.height - player->radius();

    //keep player inside its court
    if (player->getPositionY() < _screenSize.height* 0.5f) {
        if (nextPosition.y > _screenSize.height* 0.5 -
player->radius()) {
            nextPosition.y = _screenSize.height* 0.5 -
player->radius();
        }
    } else {
        if (nextPosition.y < _screenSize.height* 0.5 +
player->radius()) {
            nextPosition.y = _screenSize.height* 0.5 +
player->radius();
        }
    }
    player->setNextPosition(nextPosition);
    player->setVector(Vec2(tap.x - player->getPositionX(),
tap.y - player->getPositionY()));
  }
}
```

We check to see if the `_touch` property stored inside the player is the being moved now. If so, we update the player's position with the touch's current position, but we check to see if the new position is valid: a player cannot move outside the screen and cannot enter its opponent's court. We also update the player's vector of movement; we'll need this when we collide the player with the puck. The vector is based on the player's displacement.

3. In `onTouchesEnded`, we add this:

```
for (auto player : _players) {
    if (player->getTouch() != nullptr && player->getTouch() ==
touch) {
        //if touch ending belongs to this player, clear it
        player->setTouch(nullptr);
        player->setVector(Vec2(0,0));
    }
}
```

We clear the `_touch` property stored inside the player if this touch is the one just ending. The player also stops moving, so its vector is set to 0. Notice that we don't need the location of the touch anymore; so in `TouchesEnded` you can skip that bit of logic.

What just happened?

When you implement logic for multitouch this is pretty much what you will have to do: store the individual touches inside either an array or individual sprites, so you can keep tracking these touches.

Now, for the heart and soul of the game—the main loop.

Time for action – adding our main loop

This is the heart of our game—the `update` method:

1. We will update the puck's velocity with a little friction applied to its vector (`0.98f`). We will store what its next position will be at the end of the iteration, if no collision occurred:

```
void GameLayer::update (float dt) {

    auto ballNextPosition = _ball->getNextPosition();
    auto ballVector = _ball->getVector();
    ballVector *=  0.98f;

    ballNextPosition.x += ballVector.x;
    ballNextPosition.y += ballVector.y;
```

2. Next comes the collision. We will check collisions with each player sprite and the ball:

```
float squared_radii = pow(_player1->radius() +
_ball->radius(), 2);
for (auto player : _players) {
  auto playerNextPosition = player->getNextPosition();
  auto playerVector = player->getVector();
  float diffx = ballNextPosition.x - player->getPositionX();
  float diffy = ballNextPosition.y - player->getPositionY();
  float distance1 = pow(diffx, 2) + pow(diffy, 2);
  float distance2 = pow(_ball->getPositionX() -
playerNextPosition.x, 2) + pow(_ball->getPositionY() -
playerNextPosition.y, 2);
```

Collisions are checked through the distance between ball and players. Two conditions will flag a collision, as illustrated in the following diagram:

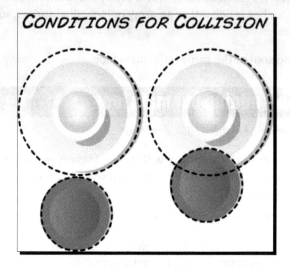

CONDITIONS FOR COLLISION

3. If the distance between ball and player equals the sum of the radii of both sprites, or is less than the sum of the radii of both sprites, we have a collision:

```
if (distance1 <= squared_radii ||
    distance2 <= squared_radii) {
```

4. We use the squared radii values so we don't need to use costly square root calculations to get the values for distance. So all values in the previous conditional statement are squared, including the distances.

5. These conditions are checked both with the player's current position and its next position, so there is less risk of the ball moving "through" the player sprite between iterations.

6. If there is a collision, we grab the magnitudes of both the ball's vector and the player's vector, and make the force with which the ball will be pushed away. We update the ball's next position in that case, and play a nice sound effect through the `SimpleAudioEngine` singleton (don't forget to include the `SimpleAudioEngine.h` header file and declare we're using the `CocosDenshion` namespace):

```
float mag_ball = pow(ballVector.x, 2) + pow(ballVector.y,
2);
float mag_player = pow(playerVector.x, 2) + pow
(playerVector.y, 2);
```

```
float force = sqrt(mag_ball + mag_player);
float angle = atan2(diffy, diffx);

    ballVector.x = force * cos(angle);
    ballVector.y = (force * sin(angle));

    ballNextPosition.x = playerNextPosition.x + (player-
    >radius() + _ball->radius() + force) * cos(angle);
    ballNextPosition.y = playerNextPosition.y + (player-
    >radius() + _ball->radius() + force) * sin(angle);

    SimpleAudioEngine::getInstance()-
    >playEffect("hit.wav");
    }
}
```

7. Next, we will check the collision between the ball and screen sides. If so, we will move the ball back to the court and play our sound effect here as well:

```
if (ballNextPosition.x < _ball->radius()) {
    ballNextPosition.x = _ball->radius();
    ballVector.x *= -0.8f;
    SimpleAudioEngine::getInstance()->playEffect("hit.wav");
}

if (ballNextPosition.x > _screenSize.width - _ball->radius()) {
    ballNextPosition.x = _screenSize.width - _ball->radius();
    ballVector.x *= -0.8f;
    SimpleAudioEngine::getInstance()->playEffect("hit.wav");
}
```

8. At the top and bottom sides of the court, we check to see whether the ball has not moved through one of the goals through our previously defined GOAL_WIDTH property as follows:

```
if (ballNextPosition.y > _screenSize.height - _ball->radius()) {
    if (_ball->getPosition().x < _screenSize.width * 0.5f -
    GOAL_WIDTH * 0.5f || _ball->getPosition().x >
    _screenSize.width * 0.5f + GOAL_WIDTH * 0.5f) {
        ballNextPosition.y = _screenSize.height - _ball-
        >radius();
        ballVector.y *= -0.8f;
        SimpleAudioEngine::getInstance()-
        >playEffect("hit.wav");
    }
}
```

```
if (ballNextPosition.y < _ball->radius() ) {
    if (_ball->getPosition().x < _screenSize.width * 0.5f -
    GOAL_WIDTH * 0.5f || _ball->getPosition().x >
    _screenSize.width * 0.5f + GOAL_WIDTH * 0.5f) {
        ballNextPosition.y = _ball->radius();
        ballVector.y *= -0.8f;
        SimpleAudioEngine::getInstance()-
        >playEffect("hit.wav");
    }
}
```

9. We finally update the ball information, and if the ball has passed through the goal posts (drum roll):

```
_ball->setVector(ballVector);
_ball->setNextPosition(ballNextPosition);

//check for goals!
if (ballNextPosition.y  < -_ball->radius() * 2) {
    this->playerScore(2);
}

if (ballNextPosition.y > _screenSize.height + _ball->radius() * 2)
{
    this->playerScore(1);
}
```

10. We call our helper method to score a point and we finish the update with the placement of all the elements, now that we know where the nextPosition value is for each one of the elements in the game:

```
_player1->setPosition(_player1->getNextPosition());
_player2->setPosition(_player2->getNextPosition());
_ball->setPosition(_ball->getNextPosition());
```

What just happened?

We have just built the game's main loop. Whenever your gameplay depends on precise collision detection, you will undoubtedly apply a similar logic of position now, position next, collision checks, and adjustments to position next, if a collision has occurred. And we finish the game with our helper method.

All that's left to do now is update the scores.

Time for action – updating scores

Time to type the last method in the game.

1. We start by playing a nice effect for a goal and stopping our ball:

```
void GameLayer::playerScore (int player) {

    SimpleAudioEngine::getInstance()->playEffect("score.wav");

    _ball->setVector(Vec2(0,0));
```

2. Then we update the score for the scoring player, updating the score label in the process. And the ball moves to the court of the player against whom a point was just scored:

```
char score_buffer[10];
if (player == 1) {
    _player1Score++;
    _player1ScoreLabel->setString(std::to_string(_player1Score));
    _ball->setNextPosition(Vec2(_screenSize.width * 0.5,
    _screenSize.height * 0.5 + 2 * _ball->radius()));

    } else {
    _player2Score++;
    _player2ScoreLabel->setString(std::to_string(_player2Score));
    _ball->setNextPosition(Vec2(_screenSize.width * 0.5,
    _screenSize.height * 0.5 - 2 * _ball->radius()));
    }
```

The players are moved to their original position and their _touch properties are cleared:

```
    _player1->setPosition(Vec2(_screenSize.width * 0.5,
    _player1->radius() * 2));
    _player2->setPosition(Vec2(_screenSize.width * 0.5,
    _screenSize.height - _player1->radius() * 2));
    _player1->setTouch(nullptr);
    _player2->setTouch(nullptr);
}
```

What just happened?

Well, guess what! You just finished your first game in Cocos2d-x. We charged forward at a brisk pace for our first game, but we managed to touch on almost every area of game development with Cocos2d-x in the process.

If you click **Run** now, you should be able to play the game. In the source code for this chapter, you should also find the complete version of the game if you run into any problems.

Time to take this to Android!

Time for action – running the game in Android

Time to deploy the game to Android.

1. Follow the instructions from the `HelloWorld` example to import the game into Eclipse.

2. Navigate to the `proj.android` folder and open the `AndroidManifest.xml` file in a text editor. Then, go to the `jni` folder and open the `Android.mk` file in a text editor.

3. In the `AndroidManifest.xml` file, edit the following line in the `activity` tag:

    ```
    android:screenOrientation="portrait"
    ```

4. And it's possible to target only tablets by adding these lines in the `supports-screens` tag:

    ```
    <supports-screens android:anyDensity="true"
                android:smallScreens="false"
                android:normalScreens="false"
                android:largeScreens="true"
                android:xlargeScreens="true"/>
    ```

5. Although if you want to target only tablets, you might also wish to target the later versions of SDK, like this:

    ```
    <uses-sdk android:minSdkVersion="11"/>
    ```

6. Next, let's edit the make file, so open the `Android.mk` file and edit the lines in `LOCAL_SRC_FILES` to read:

    ```
    LOCAL_SRC_FILES := hellocpp/main.cpp \
                    ../../Classes/AppDelegate.cpp \
                    ../../Classes/GameSprite.cpp \
                    ../../Classes/GameLayer.cpp
    ```

7. Save it and run your application (don't forget to connect an Android device, in this case, a tablet if you used the settings as explained here).

What just happened?

And that's it! You can edit these files inside Eclipse as well.

When you build a Cocos2d-x project in the command line, you see a message saying that the `hellocpp` target is being renamed. But I think this is still a bug in the build script and usually correcting that in the make file and the folder structure creates a much bigger headache. So for now, stick to the strangely named `hellocpp` in `Android.mk`.

Have a go hero

Make any changes to the code. For instance, add an extra label and then publish again from Eclipse. You may find that working with the project in this IDE is faster than Xcode.

Sadly, sooner or later, Eclipse will throw one of its infamous tantrums. A common problem that occurs if you have many projects open in your navigator is for one or many of the projects to report an error like **Cannot find the class file for java.lang.Object** or **The type java.lang.Object cannot be resolved**. Get into the habit of cleaning your project and building it as soon as you open Eclipse and keeping only active projects opened, but even that might fail you. The solution? Restart Eclipse, or better yet, delete the project from the navigator (but not from the disk!) and reimport it. Yeah, I know. Welcome to Eclipse!

Summary

You now know how to add sprites and labels, and how to add support for two screen resolutions as well as support for multitouch. There are quite a few ways to create sprites other than by passing it an image filename, and I'll show examples of these in the games to come.

`LabelTTF` won't be used as much in this book. Generally, they are good for large chunks of text and text that is not updated too frequently; we'll use bitmap fonts from now on.

So, let's move on to the next game and animations. I promise I won't make you type as much. You should get your friend to do it for you!

4

Fun with Sprites – Sky Defense

Time to build our second game! This time, you will get acquainted with the power of actions in Cocos2d-x. I'll show you how an entire game could be built just by running the various action commands contained in Cocos2d-x to make your sprites move, rotate, scale, fade, blink, and so on. And you can also use actions to animate your sprites using multiple images, like in a movie. So let's get started.

In this chapter, you will learn:

- ◆ How to optimize the development of your game with sprite sheets
- ◆ How to use bitmap fonts in your game
- ◆ How easy it is to implement and run actions
- ◆ How to scale, rotate, swing, move, and fade out a sprite
- ◆ How to load multiple `.png` files and use them to animate a sprite
- ◆ How to create a universal game with Cocos2d-x

The game – sky defense

Meet our stressed-out city of...your name of choice here. It's a beautiful day when suddenly the sky begins to fall. There are meteors rushing toward the city and it is your job to keep it safe.

The player in this game can tap the screen to start growing a bomb. When the bomb is big enough to be activated, the player taps the screen again to detonate it. Any nearby meteor will explode into a million pieces. The bigger the bomb, the bigger the detonation, and the more meteors can be taken out by it. But the bigger the bomb, the longer it takes to grow it.

But it's not just bad news coming down. There are also health packs dropping from the sky and if you allow them to reach the ground, you'll recover some of your energy.

The game settings

This is a universal game. It is designed for the iPad retina screen and it will be scaled down to fit all the other screens. The game will be played in landscape mode, and it will not need to support multitouch.

The start project

Go ahead and download the file `4198_04_START_PROJECT.zip` from this book's support page (`www.packtpub.com/support`). When you uncompress the file, you will find the basic project already set up and ready for you to work on.

The steps involved in creating this project are similar to the ones I showed you in our previous game. The command line I used was:

```
cocos new SkyDefense -p com.rengelbert.SkyDefense -l cpp -d /Users/
rengelbert/Desktop/SkyDefense
```

In Xcode you must set the **Devices** field in **Deployment Info** to **Universal**, and the **Device Family** field is set to **Universal**. And in `RootViewController.mm`, the supported interface orientation is set to **Landscape**.

The game we are going to build requires only one class, `GameLayer.cpp`, and you will find that the interface for this class already contains all the information it needs.

Also, some of the more trivial or old-news logic is already in place in the implementation file as well. But I'll go over this as we work on the game.

Adding screen support for a universal app

In the previous game, we targeted iPad size screens only. Now things get a bit more complicated as we add support for smaller screens in our universal game, as well as some of the most common Android screen sizes.

So open `AppDelegate.cpp`. Inside the `applicationDidFinishLaunching` method, we now have the following code:

```
auto screenSize = glview->getFrameSize();
auto designSize = Size(2048, 1536);
glview->setDesignResolutionSize(designSize.width, designSize.height,
ResolutionPolicy::EXACT_FIT);
std::vector<std::string> searchPaths;
if (screenSize.height > 768) {
   searchPaths.push_back("ipadhd");
   director->setContentScaleFactor(1536/designSize.height);
} else if (screenSize.height > 320) {
   searchPaths.push_back("ipad");
   director->setContentScaleFactor(768/designSize.height);
} else {
   searchPaths.push_back("iphone");
   director->setContentScaleFactor(380/designSize.height);
}
auto fileUtils = FileUtils::getInstance();
fileUtils->setSearchPaths(searchPaths);
```

Once again, we tell our `GLView` object (our OpenGL view) that we designed the game for a certain screen size (the iPad retina screen) and once again, we want our game screen to resize to match the screen on the device (`ResolutionPolicy::EXACT_FIT`).

Then we determine where to load our images from, based on the device's screen size. We have art for iPad retina, then for regular iPad which is shared by iPhone retina, and for the regular iPhone.

We end by setting the scale factor based on the designed target.

Adding background music

Still inside `AppDelegate.cpp`, we load the sound files we'll use in the game, including a `background.mp3` (courtesy of Kevin MacLeod from `incompetech.com`), which we load through the command:

```
auto audioEngine = SimpleAudioEngine::getInstance();

audioEngine->preloadBackgroundMusic(fileUtils->fullPathForFilename("backg
round.mp3").c_str());
```

We end by setting the effects' volume down a tad:

```
//lower playback volume for effects
audioEngine->setEffectsVolume(0.4f);
```

For background music volume, you must use setBackgroundMusicVolume. If you create some sort of volume control in your game, these are the calls you would make to adjust the volume based on the user's preference.

Initializing the game

Now back to GameLayer.cpp. If you take a look inside our init method, you will see that the game initializes by calling three methods: createGameScreen, createPools, and createActions.

We'll create all our screen elements inside the first method, and then create object pools so we don't instantiate any sprite inside the main loop; and we'll create all the main actions used in our game inside the createActions method.

And as soon as the game initializes, we start playing the background music, with its should loop parameter set to true:

```
SimpleAudioEngine::getInstance()-
    >playBackgroundMusic("background.mp3", true);
```

We once again store the screen size for future reference, and we'll use a _running Boolean for game states.

If you run the game now, you should only see the background image:

Using sprite sheets in Cocos2d-x

A sprite sheet is a way to group multiple images together in one image file. In order to texture a sprite with one of these images, you must have the information of where in the sprite sheet that particular image is found (its rectangle).

Sprite sheets are often organized in two files: the image one and a data file that describes where in the image you can find the individual textures.

I used `TexturePacker` to create these files for the game. You can find them inside the `ipad`, `ipadhd`, and `iphone` folders inside `Resources`. There is a `sprite_sheet.png` file for the image and a `sprite_sheet.plist` file that describes the individual frames inside the image.

This is what the `sprite_sheet.png` file looks like:

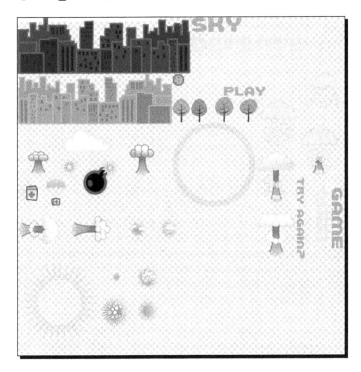

Batch drawing sprites

In Cocos2d-x, sprite sheets can be used in conjunction with a specialized node, called `SpriteBatchNode`. This node can be used whenever you wish to use multiple sprites that share the same source image inside the same node. So you could have multiple instances of a `Sprite` class that uses a `bullet.png` texture for instance. And if the source image is a sprite sheet, you can have multiple instances of sprites displaying as many different textures as you could pack inside your sprite sheet.

With `SpriteBatchNode`, you can substantially reduce the number of calls during the rendering stage of your game, which will help when targeting less powerful systems, though not noticeably in more modern devices.

Let me show you how to create a `SpriteBatchNode`.

Time for action – creating SpriteBatchNode

Let's begin implementing the `createGameScreen` method in `GameLayer.cpp`. Just below the lines that add the `bg` sprite, we instantiate our batch node:

```
void GameLayer::createGameScreen() {

  //add bg
  auto bg = Sprite::create("bg.png");
  ...

  SpriteFrameCache::getInstance()->
  addSpriteFramesWithFile("sprite_sheet.plist");

  _gameBatchNode = SpriteBatchNode::create("sprite_sheet.png");
  this->addChild(_gameBatchNode);
```

In order to create the batch node from a sprite sheet, we first load all the frame information described by the `sprite_sheet.plist` file into `SpriteFrameCache`. And then we create the batch node with the `sprite_sheet.png` file, which is the source texture shared by all sprites added to this batch node. (The background image is not part of the sprite sheet, so it's added separately before we add `_gameBatchNode` to GameLayer.)

Now we can start putting stuff inside `_gameBatchNode`.

1. First, the city:
    ```
    for (int i = 0; i < 2; i++) {
      auto sprite = Sprite::createWithSpriteFrameName
      ("city_dark.png");
        sprite->setAnchorPoint(Vec2(0.5,0));
      sprite->setPosition(_screenSize.width * (0.25f + i *
    0.5f),0));
      _gameBatchNode->addChild(sprite, kMiddleground);

      sprite = Sprite::createWithSpriteFrameName
      ("city_light.png");
      sprite->setAnchorPoint(Vec2(0.5,0));
      sprite->setPosition(Vec2(_screenSize.width * (0.25f + i *
    0.5f),
      _screenSize.height * 0.1f));
      _gameBatchNode->addChild(sprite, kBackground);
    }
    ```

2. Then the trees:

```
//add trees
for (int i = 0; i < 3; i++) {
  auto sprite = Sprite::createWithSpriteFrameName("trees.png");
  sprite->setAnchorPoint(Vec2(0.5f, 0.0f));
  sprite->setPosition(Vec2(_screenSize.width * (0.2f + i *
0.3f),0));
  _gameBatchNode->addChild(sprite, kForeground);


}
```

Notice that here we create sprites by passing it a sprite frame name. The IDs for these frame names were loaded into `SpriteFrameCache` through our `sprite_sheet.plist` file.

3. The screen so far is made up of two instances of `city_dark.png` tiling at the bottom of the screen, and two instances of `city_light.png` also tiling. One needs to appear on top of the other and for that we use the enumerated values declared in `GameLayer.h`:

```
enum {
  kBackground,
  kMiddleground,
  kForeground
};
```

4. We use the `addChild( Node, zOrder)` method to layer our sprites on top of each other, using different values for their z order.

So for example, when we later add three sprites showing the `trees.png` sprite frame, we add them on top of all previous sprites using the highest value for z that we find in the enumerated list, which is `kForeground`.

 Why go through the trouble of tiling the images and not using one large image instead, or combining some of them with the background image? Because I wanted to include the greatest number of images possible inside the one sprite sheet, and have that sprite sheet to be as small as possible, to illustrate all the clever ways you can use and optimize sprite sheets. This is not necessary in this particular game.

What just happened?

We began creating the initial screen for our game. We are using a `SpriteBatchNode` to contain all the sprites that use images from our sprite sheet. So `SpriteBatchNode` behaves as any node does—as a container. And we can layer individual sprites inside the batch node by manipulating their z order.

Bitmap fonts in Cocos2d-x

The Cocos2d-x `Label` class has a static `create` method that uses bitmap images for the characters.

The bitmap image we are using here was created with the program GlyphDesigner, and in essence, it works just as a sprite sheet does. As a matter of fact, `Label` extends `SpriteBatchNode`, so it behaves just like a batch node.

You have images for all individual characters you'll need packed inside a PNG file (`font.png`), and then a data file (`font.fnt`) describing where each character is. The following screenshot shows how the font sprite sheet looks like for our game:

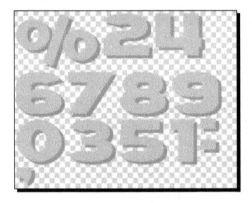

The difference between `Label` and a regular `SpriteBatchNode` class is that the data file also feeds the `Label` object information on how to *write* with this font. In other words, how to space out the characters and lines correctly.

The `Label` objects we are using in the game are instantiated with the name of the data file and their initial string value:

```
_scoreDisplay = Label::createWithBMFont("font.fnt", "0");
```

And the value for the label is changed through the `setString` method:

```
_scoreDisplay->setString("1000");
```

Just as with every other image in the game, we also have different versions of font.fnt and font.png in our Resources folders, one for each screen definition. FileUtils will once again do the heavy lifting of finding the correct file for the correct screen.

So now let's create the labels for our game.

Time for action – creating bitmap font labels

Creating a bitmap font is somewhat similar to creating a batch node.

1. Continuing with our createGameScreen method, add the following lines to the score label:

```
_scoreDisplay = Label::createWithBMFont("font.fnt", "0");
_scoreDisplay->setAnchorPoint(Vec2(1,0.5));
_scoreDisplay->setPosition(Vec2
  (_screenSize.width * 0.8f, _screenSize.height * 0.94f));
this->addChild(_scoreDisplay);
```

And then add a label to display the energy level, and set its horizontal alignment to Right:

```
_energyDisplay = Label::createWithBMFont("font.fnt", "100%",
TextHAlignment::RIGHT);
_energyDisplay->setPosition(Vec2
  (_screenSize.width * 0.3f, _screenSize.height * 0.94f));
this->addChild(_energyDisplay);
```

2. Add the following line for an icon that appears next to the _energyDisplay label:

```
auto icon = Sprite::createWithSpriteFrameName
  ("health_icon.png");
icon->setPosition( Vec2(_screenSize.
  width * 0.15f, _screenSize.height * 0.94f) );
_gameBatchNode->addChild(icon, kBackground);
```

What just happened?

We just created our first bitmap font object in Cocos2d-x. Now let's finish creating our game's sprites.

Time for action – adding the final screen sprites

The last sprites we need to create are the clouds, the bomb and shockwave, and our game state messages.

1. Back to the `createGameScreen` method, add the clouds to the screen:

    ```
    for (int i = 0; i < 4; i++) {
        float cloud_y = i % 2 == 0 ? _screenSize.height * 0.4f : _
    screenSize.height * 0.5f;
        auto cloud = Sprite::createWithSpriteFrameName("cloud.png");
        cloud->setPosition(Vec2 (_screenSize.width * 0.1f + i * _
    screenSize.width * 0.3f,  cloud_y));
        _gameBatchNode->addChild(cloud, kBackground);
        _clouds.pushBack(cloud);
    }
    ```

2. Create the `_bomb` sprite; players will *grow* when tapping the screen:

    ```
    _bomb = Sprite::createWithSpriteFrameName("bomb.png");
    _bomb->getTexture()->generateMipmap();
    _bomb->setVisible(false);

    auto size = _bomb->getContentSize();

    //add sparkle inside bomb sprite
    auto sparkle = Sprite::createWithSpriteFrameName("sparkle.png");
    sparkle->setPosition(Vec2(size.width * 0.72f, size.height *
      0.72f));
    _bomb->addChild(sparkle, kMiddleground, kSpriteSparkle);

    //add halo inside bomb sprite
    auto halo = Sprite::createWithSpriteFrameName
      ("halo.png");
    halo->setPosition(Vec2(size.width * 0.4f, size.height *
      0.4f));
    _bomb->addChild(halo, kMiddleground, kSpriteHalo);
    _gameBatchNode->addChild(_bomb, kForeground);
    ```

3. Then create the `_shockwave` sprite that appears after the `_bomb` goes off:

    ```
    _shockWave = Sprite::createWithSpriteFrameName
      ("shockwave.png");
    _shockWave->getTexture()->generateMipmap();
    _shockWave->setVisible(false);
    _gameBatchNode->addChild(_shockWave);
    ```

4. Finally, add the two messages that appear on the screen, one for our `intro` state and one for our `gameover` state:

```
_introMessage = Sprite::createWithSpriteFrameName
  ("logo.png");
_introMessage->setPosition(Vec2
  (_screenSize.width * 0.5f, _screenSize.height * 0.6f));
_introMessage->setVisible(true);
this->addChild(_introMessage, kForeground);

_gameOverMessage = Sprite::createWithSpriteFrameName
  ("gameover.png");
_gameOverMessage->setPosition(Vec2
  (_screenSize.width * 0.5f, _screenSize.height * 0.65f));
_gameOverMessage->setVisible(false);
this->addChild(_gameOverMessage, kForeground);
```

What just happened?

There is a lot of new information regarding sprites in the previous code. So let's go over it carefully:

- We started by adding the clouds. We put the sprites inside a vector so we can move the clouds later. Notice that they are also part of our batch node.

- Next comes the bomb sprite and our first new call:

  ```
  _bomb->getTexture()->generateMipmap();
  ```

- With this we are telling the framework to create antialiased copies of this texture in diminishing sizes (mipmaps), since we are going to scale it down later. This is optional of course; sprites can be resized without first generating mipmaps, but if you notice loss of quality in your scaled sprites, you can fix that by creating mipmaps for their texture.

> The texture must have size values in so-called POT (power of 2: 2, 4, 8, 16, 32, 64, 128, 256, 512, 1024, 2048, and so on). Textures in OpenGL must always be sized this way; when they are not, Cocos2d-x will do one of two things: it will either resize the texture in memory, adding transparent pixels until the image reaches a POT size, or stop the execution on an assert. With textures used for mipmaps, the framework will stop execution for non-POT textures.

- ◆ I add the `sparkle` and the `halo` sprites as children to the `_bomb` sprite. This will use the container characteristic of nodes to our advantage. When I grow the bomb, all its children will grow with it.

- ◆ Notice too that I use a third parameter to `addChild` for `halo` and `sparkle`:

```
bomb->addChild(halo, kMiddleground, kSpriteHalo);
```

- ◆ This third parameter is an integer tag from yet another enumerated list declared in `GameLayer.h`. I can use this tag to retrieve a particular child from a sprite as follows:

```
auto halo = (Sprite *)
   bomb->getChildByTag(kSpriteHalo);
```

We now have our game screen in place:

Next come object pools.

Time for action – creating our object pools

The pools are just vectors of objects. And here are the steps to create them:

1. Inside the `createPools` method, we first create a pool for meteors:

```
void GameLayer::createPools() {
    int i;
    _meteorPoolIndex = 0;
    for (i = 0; i < 50; i++) {
    auto sprite = Sprite::createWithSpriteFrameName("meteor.png");
    sprite->setVisible(false);
    _gameBatchNode->addChild(sprite, kMiddleground, kSpriteMeteor);
    _meteorPool.pushBack(sprite);
    }
}
```

2. Then we create an object pool for health packs:

```
    _healthPoolIndex = 0;
    for (i = 0; i < 20; i++) {
        auto sprite = Sprite::createWithSpriteFrameName("health.png");
        sprite->setVisible(false);
        sprite->setAnchorPoint(Vec2(0.5f, 0.8f));
        _gameBatchNode->addChild(sprite, kMiddleground, kSpriteHealth);
        _healthPool.pushBack(sprite);
    }
```

3. We'll use the corresponding pool index to retrieve objects from the vectors as the game progresses.

What just happened?

We now have a vector of invisible meteor sprites and a vector of invisible health sprites. We'll use their respective pool indices to retrieve these from the vector as needed as you'll see in a moment. But first we need to take care of actions and animations.

 With object pools, we reduce the number of instantiations during the main loop, and it allows us to never destroy anything that can be reused. But if you need to remove a child from a node, use `->removeChild` or `->removeChildByTag` if a tag is present.

Actions in a nutshell

If you remember, a node will store information about position, scale, rotation, visibility, and opacity of a node. And in Cocos2d-x, there is an `Action` class to change each one of these values over time, in effect animating these transformations.

Actions are usually created with a static method `create`. The majority of these actions are time-based, so usually the first parameter you need to pass an action is the time length for the action. So for instance:

```
auto fadeout = FadeOut::create(1.0f);
```

This creates a `fadeout` action that will take one second to complete. You can run it on a sprite, or node, as follows:

```
mySprite->runAction(fadeout);
```

Cocos2d-x has an incredibly flexible system that allows us to create any combination of actions and transformations to achieve any effect we desire.

You may, for instance, choose to create an action sequence (`Sequence`) that contains more than one action; or you can apply easing effects (`EaseIn`, `EaseOut`, and so on) to your actions. You can choose to repeat an action a certain number of times (`Repeat`) or forever (`RepeatForever`); and you can add callbacks to functions you want called once an action is completed (usually inside a `Sequence` action).

Time for action – creating actions with Cocos2d-x

Creating actions with Cocos2d-x is a very simple process:

1. Inside our `createActions` method, we will instantiate the actions we can use repeatedly in our game. Let's create our first actions:

```
void GameLayer::createActions() {
 //swing action for health drops
 auto easeSwing = Sequence::create(
 EaseInOut::create(RotateTo::create(1.2f, -10), 2),
 EaseInOut::create(RotateTo::create(1.2f, 10), 2),
 nullptr);//mark the end of a sequence with a nullptr
 _swingHealth = RepeatForever::create( (ActionInterval *)
easeSwing );
 _swingHealth->retain();
```

2. Actions can be combined in many different forms. Here, the retained `_swingHealth` action is a `RepeatForever` action of `Sequence` that will rotate the health sprite first one way, then the other, with `EaseInOut` wrapping the `RotateTo` action. `RotateTo` takes `1.2` seconds to rotate the sprite first to `-10` degrees and then to `10`. And the easing has a value of `2`, which I suggest you experiment with to get a sense of what it means visually. Next we add three more actions:

```
//action sequence for shockwave: fade out, callback when
//done
_shockwaveSequence = Sequence::create(
  FadeOut::create(1.0f),
  CallFunc::create(std::bind(&GameLayer::shockwaveDone, this)),
nullptr);
_shockwaveSequence->retain();

//action to grow bomb
_growBomb = ScaleTo::create(6.0f, 1.0);
_growBomb->retain();

//action to rotate sprites
auto rotate = RotateBy::create(0.5f , -90);
_rotateSprite = RepeatForever::create( rotate );
_rotateSprite->retain();
```

3. First, another `Sequence`. This will fade out the sprite and call the `shockwaveDone` function, which is already implemented in the class and turns the `_shockwave` sprite invisible when called.

4. The last one is a `RepeatForever` action of a `RotateBy` action. In half a second, the sprite running this action will rotate `-90` degrees and will do that again and again.

What just happened?

You just got your first glimpse of how to create actions in Cocos2d-x and how the framework allows for all sorts of combinations to accomplish any effect.

It may be hard at first to read through a `Sequence` action and understand what's happening, but the logic is easy to follow once you break it down into its individual parts.

But we are not done with the `createActions` method yet. Next come sprite animations.

Animating a sprite in Cocos2d-x

The key thing to remember is that an animation is just another type of action, one that changes the texture used by a sprite over a period of time.

In order to create an animation action, you need to first create an `Animation` object. This object will store all the information regarding the different sprite frames you wish to use in the animation, the length of the animation in seconds, and whether it loops or not.

With this `Animation` object, you then create a `Animate` action. Let's take a look.

Time for action – creating animations

Animations are a specialized type of action that require a few extra steps:

1. Inside the same `createActions` method, add the lines for the two animations we have in the game. First, we start with the animation that shows an explosion when a meteor reaches the city. We begin by loading the frames into an `Animation` object:

```
auto animation = Animation::create();
int i;
for(i = 1; i <= 10; i++) {
   auto name = String::createWithFormat("boom%i.png", i);
   auto frame = SpriteFrameCache::getInstance()-
>getSpriteFrameByName(name->getCString());
   animation->addSpriteFrame(frame);
}
```

2. Then we use the `Animation` object inside a `Animate` action:

```
animation->setDelayPerUnit(1 / 10.0f);
animation->setRestoreOriginalFrame(true);
_groundHit =
   Sequence::create(
      MoveBy::create(0, Vec2(0,_screenSize.height * 0.12f)),
      Animate::create(animation),
      CallFuncN::create(CC_CALLBACK_1(GameLayer::animationDone,
this)), nullptr);
_groundHit->retain();
```

3. The same steps are repeated to create the other explosion animation used when the player hits a meteor or a health pack.

```
animation = Animation::create();
for(int i = 1; i <= 7; i++) {
```

```
    auto name = String::createWithFormat("explosion_small%i.png", i);
    auto frame = SpriteFrameCache::getInstance()-
>getSpriteFrameByName(name->getCString());
    animation->addSpriteFrame(frame);
}

animation->setDelayPerUnit(0.5 / 7.0f);
animation->setRestoreOriginalFrame(true);
_explosion = Sequence::create(
      Animate::create(animation),
    CallFuncN::create(CC_CALLBACK_1(GameLayer::animationDone,
this)), nullptr);
_explosion->retain();
```

What just happened?

We created two instances of a very special kind of action in Cocos2d-x: `Animate`. Here is what we did:

- First, we created an `Animation` object. This object holds the references to all the textures used in the animation. The frames were named in such a way that they could easily be concatenated inside a loop (`boom1`, `boom2`, `boom3`, and so on). There are 10 frames for the first animation and seven for the second.

- The textures (or frames) are `SpriteFrame` objects we grab from `SpriteFrameCache`, which as you remember, contains all the information from the `sprite_sheet.plist` data file. So the frames are in our sprite sheet.

- Then when all frames are in place, we determine the delay of each frame by dividing the total amount of seconds we want the animation to last by the total number of frames.

- The `setRestoreOriginalFrame` method is important here. If we set `setRestoreOriginalFrame` to `true`, then the sprite will revert to its original appearance once the animation is over. For example, if I have an explosion animation that will run on a meteor sprite, then by the end of the explosion animation, the sprite will revert to displaying the meteor texture.

- Time for the actual action. `Animate` receives the `Animation` object as its parameter. (In the first animation, we shift the position of the sprite just before the explosion appears, so there is an extra `MoveBy` method.)

- And in both instances, I make a call to an `animationDone` callback already implemented in the class. It makes the calling sprite invisible:

```
void GameLayer::animationDone (Node* pSender) {
  pSender->setVisible(false);
}
```

> We could have used the same method for both callbacks (`animationDone` and `shockwaveDone`) as they accomplish the same thing. But I wanted to show you a callback that receives as an argument, the node that made the call and one that did not. Respectively, these are `CallFuncN` and `CallFunc`, and were used inside the action sequences we just created.

Time to make our game tick!

Okay, we have our main elements in place and are ready to add the final bit of logic to run the game. But how will everything work?

We will use a system of countdowns to add new meteors and new health packs, as well as a countdown that will incrementally make the game harder to play.

On touch, the player will start the game if the game is not running, and also add bombs and explode them during gameplay. An explosion creates a shockwave.

On update, we will check against collision between our `_shockwave` sprite (if visible) and all our falling objects. And that's it. Cocos2d-x will take care of all the rest through our created actions and callbacks!

So let's implement our touch events first.

Time for action – handling touches

Time to bring the player to our party:

1. Time to implement our `onTouchBegan` method. We'll begin by handling the two game states, `intro` and `game over`:

```
bool GameLayer::onTouchBegan
  (Touch * touch, Event * event){

    //if game not running, we are seeing either intro or
  //gameover
    if (!_running) {
      //if intro, hide intro message
      if (_introMessage->isVisible()) {
        _introMessage->setVisible(false);

        //if game over, hide game over message
      } else if (_gameOverMessage->isVisible()) {
```

```
        SimpleAudioEngine::getInstance()->stopAllEffects();
        _gameOverMessage->setVisible(false);

    }

    this->resetGame();
    return true;
  }
```

2. Here we check to see if the game is not running. If not, we check to see if
    any of our messages are visible. If _introMessage is visible, we hide it. If
    _gameOverMessage is visible, we stop all current sound effects and hide the
    message as well. Then we call a method called resetGame, which will reset
    all the game data (energy, score, and countdowns) to their initial values, and set
    _running to true.

3. Next we handle the touches. But we only need to handle one each time so we use
    ->anyObject() on Set:

```
auto touch = (Touch *)pTouches->anyObject();

if (touch) {

  //if bomb already growing...
  if (_bomb->isVisible()) {
    //stop all actions on bomb, halo and sparkle
    _bomb->stopAllActions();
    auto child = (Sprite *) _bomb->getChildByTag(kSpriteHalo);
    child->stopAllActions();
    child = (Sprite *) _bomb->getChildByTag(kSpriteSparkle);
    child->stopAllActions();

    //if bomb is the right size, then create shockwave
    if (_bomb->getScale() > 0.3f) {
      _shockWave->setScale(0.1f);
      _shockWave->setPosition(_bomb->getPosition());
      _shockWave->setVisible(true);
      _shockWave->runAction(ScaleTo::create(0.5f, _bomb-
>getScale() * 2.0f));
      _shockWave->runAction(_shockwaveSequence->clone());
      SimpleAudioEngine::getInstance()->playEffect("bombRelease.
wav");

    } else {
```

```
        SimpleAudioEngine::getInstance()->playEffect("bombFail.
wav");
    }
    _bomb->setVisible(false);
    //reset hits with shockwave, so we can count combo hits
    _shockwaveHits = 0;

  //if no bomb currently on screen, create one
  } else {
      Point tap = touch->getLocation();
      _bomb->stopAllActions();
      _bomb->setScale(0.1f);
      _bomb->setPosition(tap);
      _bomb->setVisible(true);
      _bomb->setOpacity(50);
      _bomb->runAction(_growBomb->clone());

      auto child = (Sprite *) _bomb->getChildByTag(kSpriteHalo);
      child->runAction(_rotateSprite->clone());
      child = (Sprite *) _bomb->getChildByTag(kSpriteSparkle);
      child->runAction(_rotateSprite->clone());
  }
}
```

4. If `_bomb` is visible, it means it's already growing on the screen. So on touch, we use the `stopAllActions()` method on the bomb and we use the `stopAllActions()` method on its children that we retrieve through our tags:

```
child = (Sprite *) _bomb->getChildByTag(kSpriteHalo);
child->stopAllActions();
child = (Sprite *) _bomb->getChildByTag(kSpriteSparkle);
child->stopAllActions();
```

5. If `_bomb` is the right size, we start our `_shockwave`. If it isn't, we play a bomb failure sound effect; there is no explosion and `_shockwave` is not made visible.

6. If we have an explosion, then the `_shockwave` sprite is set to 10 percent of the scale. It's placed at the same spot as the bomb, and we run a couple of actions on it: we grow the `_shockwave` sprite to twice the scale the bomb was when it went off and we run a copy of `_shockwaveSequence` that we created earlier.

7. Finally, if no `_bomb` is currently visible on screen, we create one. And we run clones of previously created actions on the `_bomb` sprite and its children. When `_bomb` grows, its children grow. But when the children rotate, the bomb does not: a parent changes its children, but the children do not change their parent.

What just happened?

We just added part of the core logic of the game. It is with touches that the player creates and explodes bombs to stop meteors from reaching the city. Now we need to create our falling objects. But first, let's set up our countdowns and our game data.

Time for action – starting and restarting the game

Let's add the logic to start and restart the game.

1. Let's write the implementation for `resetGame`:

```
void GameLayer::resetGame(void) {
    _score = 0;
    _energy = 100;

    //reset timers and "speeds"
    _meteorInterval = 2.5;
    _meteorTimer = _meteorInterval * 0.99f;
    _meteorSpeed = 10;//in seconds to reach ground
    _healthInterval = 20;
    _healthTimer = 0;
    _healthSpeed = 15;//in seconds to reach ground

    _difficultyInterval = 60;
    _difficultyTimer = 0;

    _running = true;

    //reset labels
    _energyDisplay->setString(std::to_string((int) _energy) +
"%");
    _scoreDisplay->setString(std::to_string((int) _score));
}
```

2. Next, add the implementation of `stopGame`:

```
void GameLayer::stopGame() {

    _running = false;

    //stop all actions currently running
    int i;
```

```
        int count = (int) _fallingObjects.size();

        for (i = count-1; i >= 0; i--) {
            auto sprite = _fallingObjects.at(i);
            sprite->stopAllActions();
            sprite->setVisible(false);
            _fallingObjects.erase(i);
        }
    if (_bomb->isVisible()) {
        _bomb->stopAllActions();
        _bomb->setVisible(false);
        auto child = _bomb->getChildByTag(kSpriteHalo);
        child->stopAllActions();
        child = _bomb->getChildByTag(kSpriteSparkle);
        child->stopAllActions();
    }
    if (_shockWave->isVisible()) {
        _shockWave->stopAllActions();
        _shockWave->setVisible(false);
    }
    if (_ufo->isVisible()) {
        _ufo->stopAllActions();
        _ufo->setVisible(false);
        auto ray = _ufo->getChildByTag(kSpriteRay);
        ray->stopAllActions();
        ray->setVisible(false);
    }
}
```

What just happened?

With these methods we control gameplay. We start the game with default values through resetGame(), and we stop all actions with stopGame().

Already implemented in the class is the method that makes the game more difficult as time progresses. If you take a look at the method (increaseDifficulty) you will see that it reduces the interval between meteors and reduces the time it takes for meteors to reach the ground.

All we need now is the update method to run the countdowns and check for collisions.

Time for action – updating the game

We already have the code that updates the countdowns inside the update. If it's time to add a meteor or a health pack we do it. If it's time to make the game more difficult to play, we do that too.

 It is possible to use an action for these timers: a Sequence action with a Delay action object and a callback. But there are advantages to using these countdowns. It's easier to reset them and to change them, and we can take them right into our main loop.

So it's time to add our main loop:

1. What we need to do is check for collisions. So add the following code:

```
if (_shockWave->isVisible()) {
 count = (int) _fallingObjects.size();
 for (i = count-1; i >= 0; i--) {
    auto sprite = _fallingObjects.at(i);
    diffx = _shockWave->getPositionX() - sprite->getPositionX();
    diffy = _shockWave->getPositionY() - sprite->getPositionY();
    if (pow(diffx, 2) + pow(diffy, 2) <= pow(_shockWave-
>getBoundingBox().size.width * 0.5f, 2)) {
      sprite->stopAllActions();
      sprite->runAction( _explosion->clone());
      SimpleAudioEngine::getInstance()->playEffect("boom.wav");
      if (sprite->getTag() == kSpriteMeteor) {
        _shockwaveHits++;
        _score += _shockwaveHits * 13 + _shockwaveHits * 2;
      }
      //play sound
      _fallingObjects.erase(i);
    }
  }
 _scoreDisplay->setString(std::to_string(_score));
}
```

2. If _shockwave is visible, we check the distance between it and each sprite in _fallingObjects vector. If we hit any meteors, we increase the value of the _shockwaveHits property so we can award the player for multiple hits. Next we move the clouds:

```
//move clouds
for (auto sprite : _clouds) {
```

```
sprite->setPositionX(sprite->getPositionX() + dt * 20);
if (sprite->getPositionX() > _screenSize.width + sprite-
>getBoundingBox().size.width * 0.5f)
    sprite->setPositionX(-sprite->getBoundingBox().size.width *
0.5f);
}
```

3. I chose not to use a `MoveTo` action for the clouds to show you the amount of code that can be replaced by a simple action. If not for Cocos2d-x actions, we would have to implement logic to move, rotate, swing, scale, and explode all our sprites!

4. And finally:

```
if (_bomb->isVisible()) {
    if (_bomb->getScale() > 0.3f) {
        if (_bomb->getOpacity() != 255)
            _bomb->setOpacity(255);
    }
}
```

5. We give the player an extra visual cue to when a bomb is ready to explode by changing its opacity.

What just happened?

The main loop is pretty straightforward when you don't have to worry about updating individual sprites, as our actions take care of that for us. We pretty much only need to run collision checks between our sprites, and to determine when it's time to throw something new at the player.

So now the only thing left to do is grab the meteors and health packs from the pools when their timers are up. So let's get right to it.

Time for action – retrieving objects from the pool

We just need to use the correct index to retrieve the objects from their respective vector:

1. To retrieve meteor sprites, we'll use the `resetMeteor` method:

```
void GameLayer::resetMeteor(void) {
    //if too many objects on screen, return
    if (_fallingObjects.size() > 30) return;

    auto meteor = _meteorPool.at(_meteorPoolIndex);
    _meteorPoolIndex++;
```

```
   if (_meteorPoolIndex == _meteorPool.size())
     _meteorPoolIndex = 0;
     int meteor_x = rand() % (int) (_screenSize.width * 0.8f) +
_screenSize.width * 0.1f;
     int meteor_target_x = rand() % (int) (_screenSize.width * 0.8f)
+ _screenSize.width * 0.1f;

   meteor->stopAllActions();
   meteor->setPosition(Vec2(meteor_x, _screenSize.height +
meteor->getBoundingBox().size.height * 0.5));

   //create action
   auto  rotate = RotateBy::create(0.5f ,  -90);
   auto  repeatRotate = RepeatForever::create( rotate );
   auto  sequence = Sequence::create (
           MoveTo::create( _meteorSpeed, Vec2(meteor_target_x,
_screenSize.height * 0.15f)),
           CallFunc::create(std::bind(&GameLayer::fallingObjec
tDone, this, meteor) ), nullptr);
  meteor->setVisible ( true );
  meteor->runAction(repeatRotate);
  meteor->runAction(sequence);
  _fallingObjects.pushBack(meteor);
}
```

2. We grab the next available meteor from the pool, then we pick a random start and end x value for its `MoveTo` action. The meteor starts at the top of the screen and will move to the bottom towards the city, but the x value is randomly picked each time.

3. We rotate the meteor inside a `RepeatForever` action, and we use `Sequence` to move the sprite to its target position and then call back `fallingObjectDone` when the meteor has reached its target. We finish by adding the new meteor we retrieved from the pool to the `_fallingObjects` vector so we can check collisions with it.

4. The method to retrieve the health (`resetHealth`) sprites is pretty much the same, except that `swingHealth` action is used instead of rotate. You'll find that method already implemented in `GameLayer.cpp`.

What just happened?

So in `resetGame` we set the timers, and we update them in the `update` method. We use these timers to add meteors and health packs to the screen by grabbing the next available one from their respective pool, and then we proceed to run collisions between an exploding bomb and these falling objects.

Notice that in both `resetMeteor` and `resetHealth` we don't add new sprites if too many are on screen already:

```
if (_fallingObjects->size() > 30) return;
```

This way the game does not get ridiculously hard, and we never run out of unused objects in our pools.

And the very last bit of logic in our game is our `fallingObjectDone` callback, called when either a meteor or a health pack has reached the ground, at which point it awards or punishes the player for letting sprites through.

When you take a look at that method inside `GameLayer.cpp`, you will notice how we use `->getTag()` to quickly ascertain which type of sprite we are dealing with (the one calling the method):

```
if (pSender->getTag() == kSpriteMeteor) {
```

If it's a meteor, we decrease energy from the player, play a sound effect, and run the explosion animation; an autorelease copy of the `_groundHit` action we retained earlier, so we don't need to repeat all that logic every time we need to run this action.

If the item is a health pack, we increase the energy or give the player some points, play a nice sound effect, and hide the sprite.

Play the game!

We've been coding like mad, and it's finally time to run the game. But first, don't forget to release all the items we retained. In `GameLayer.cpp`, add our destructor method:

```
GameLayer::~GameLayer () {

    //release all retained actions
    CC_SAFE_RELEASE(_growBomb);
    CC_SAFE_RELEASE(_rotateSprite);
    CC_SAFE_RELEASE(_shockwaveSequence);
    CC_SAFE_RELEASE(_swingHealth);
    CC_SAFE_RELEASE(_groundHit);
    CC_SAFE_RELEASE(_explosion);
    CC_SAFE_RELEASE(_ufoAnimation);
    CC_SAFE_RELEASE(_blinkRay);

    _clouds.clear();
    _meteorPool.clear();
    _healthPool.clear();
    _fallingObjects.clear();
}
```

The actual game screen will now look something like this:

Once again, you can refer to 4198_04_FINAL_PROJECT.zip if you find any problems running the code.

Now, let's take this to Android.

Time for action – running the game in Android

Follow these steps to deploy the game to Android:

1. This time, there is no need to alter the manifest because the default settings are the ones we want. So, navigate to proj.android and then to the jni folder and open the Android.mk file in a text editor.

2. Edit the lines in LOCAL_SRC_FILES to read as follows:

```
LOCAL_SRC_FILES := hellocpp/main.cpp \
                   ../../Classes/AppDelegate.cpp \
                   ../../Classes/GameLayer.cpp
```

3. Follow the instructions from the HelloWorld and AirHockey examples to import the game into Eclipse.

4. Save it and run your application. This time, you can try out different size screens if you have the devices.

What just happened?

You just ran a universal app in Android. And nothing could have been simpler.

As a bonus, I've added another version of the game with an extra type of enemy to deal with: a UFO hell-bent on zapping the city! You may find this in `4198_04_BONUS_PROJECT.zip`.

Pop quiz – sprites and actions

Q1. A `SpriteBatchNode` can contain what types of elements?

1. Sprites using textures from two or more sprite sheets.
2. Sprites using the same source texture.
3. Blank sprites.
4. Sprites using textures from one sprite sheet and one other image.

Q2. In order to run an action nonstop, what do I need to use?

1. `RepeatForever`.
2. `Repeat`.
3. The default behavior of an action is to run nonstop.
4. Actions can't repeat forever.

Q3. In order to animate a sprite so that it would move to a certain point on the screen and then fade out, what actions would I need?

1. A `Sequence` listing an `EaseIn` and `EaseOut` action.
2. A `Sequence` listing a `FadeOut` and `MoveTo` action.
3. A `Sequence` listing a `MoveTo` or `MoveBy` and a `FadeOut` action.
4. A `Sequence` listing a `RotateBy` and `FadeOut` action.

Q4. To create a sprite frame animation, what group of classes are absolutely essential?

1. `Sprite`, `SpriteBatchNode`, and `EaseIn`.
2. `SpriteFrameCache`, `RotateBy`, and `ActionManager`.
3. `Sprite`, `Layer`, and `FadeOut`.
4. `SpriteFrame`, `Animation`, and `Animate`.

Summary

In my opinion, after nodes and all their derived objects, actions are the second best thing about Cocos2d-x. They are time savers and can quickly spice things up in any project with professional-looking animations. And I hope with the examples found in this chapter, and along with the ones found in the Cocos2d-x samples test project, you will be able to create any action you need with Cocos2d-x.

In the next chapter, I'll introduce you to another simple way you can spice things up in your game: with particles!

5
On the Line – Rocket Through

In our third game, Rocket Through, we'll use particle effects to spice things up a bit, and we'll use DrawNode to make our own OpenGL drawings on screen. And be advised, this game uses quite a bit of vector math, but luckily for us, Cocos2d-x comes bundled with a sweet pack of helper methods to deal with that as well.

You will learn:

- How to load and set up a particle system
- How to draw primitives (lines, circles, and more) with `DrawNode`
- How to use vector math helper methods included in Cocos2d-x

The game – Rocket Through

In this sci-fi version of the classic Snake game engine, you control a rocket ship that must move around seven planets, collecting tiny supernovas. But here's the catch: you can only steer the rocket by rotating it around pivot points put in place through `touch` events. So the vector of movement we set for the rocket ship is at times linear and at times circular.

The game settings

This is a universal game designed for the regular iPad and then scaled up and down to match the screen resolution of other devices. It is set to play in portrait mode and it does not support multitouches.

Play first, work later

Download the `4198_05_START_PROJECT.zip` and `4198_05_FINAL_PROJECT.zip` files from this book's **Support** page.

You will, once again, use the **Start Project** option to work on; this way, you won't need to type logic or syntax already covered in previous chapters. The **Start Project** option contains all the resource files and all the class declarations as well as placeholders for all the methods inside the classes' implementation files. We'll go over these in a moment.

You should run the final project version to acquaint yourself with the game. By pressing and dragging your finger on the rocket ship, you draw a line. Release the touch and you create a pivot point. The ship will rotate around this pivot point until you press on the ship again to release it. Your aim is to collect the bright supernovas and avoid the planets.

The start project

If you run the **Start Project** option, you should see the basic game screen already in place. There is no need to repeat the steps we've taken in our previous tutorial to create a batch node and place all the screen sprites. We once again have a `_gameBatchNode` object and a `createGameScreen` method.

But by all means, read through the code inside the `createGameScreen` method. What is of key importance here is that each planet we create is stored inside the `_planets` vector. And we also create our `_rocket` object (the `Rocket` class) and our `_lineContainer` object (the `LineContainer` class) here. More on these soon.

In the **Start Project** option, we also have our old friend `GameSprite`, which extends `Sprite` here with an extra method to get the `radius()` method of our sprites. The `Rocket` object and all the planets are `GameSprite` objects.

Screen settings

So if you have the **Start Project** option opened in Xcode, let's review the screen settings for this game in `AppDelegate.cpp`. Inside the `applicationDidFinishLaunching` method, you should see this:

```
auto designSize = Size(1536, 2048);

glview->setDesignResolutionSize(designSize.width, designSize.height,
ResolutionPolicy::EXACT_FIT);

std::vector<std::string> searchPaths;
if (screenSize.width > 768) {
  searchPaths.push_back("ipadhd");
  director->setContentScaleFactor(1536/designSize.width);
} else if (screenSize.width > 320) {
  searchPaths.push_back("ipad");
  director->setContentScaleFactor(768/designSize.width);
} else {
  searchPaths.push_back("iphone");
  director->setContentScaleFactor(380/designSize.width);
}
auto fileUtils = FileUtils::getInstance();
fileUtils->setSearchPaths(searchPaths);
```

So we basically start the same way we did in the previous game. The majority of sprites in this game are circle-shaped and you may notice some distortion in different screens; you should test the same configuration but using different `ResolutionPolicies`, such as `SHOW_ALL`.

So what are particles?

Particles or particle systems are a way to add special effects to your applications. In general terms this is achieved by the use of a large number of tiny textured sprites (particles), which are animated and run through a series of transformations. You can use these systems to create smoke, explosions, sparks, lightening, rain, snow, and other such effects.

As I mentioned in *Chapter 1, Installing Cocos2d-x*, you should seriously consider getting yourself a program to help you design your particle systems. In this game, the particles were created in ParticleDesigner.

It's time to add them to our game!

Time for action – creating particle systems

For particles, all we need is the XML file describing the particle system's properties.

1. So let's go to GameLayer.cpp.

2. The game initializes by calling createGameScreen, which is already in place, then createParticles and createStarGrid, which is also implemented. So let's go over the createParticles method now.

3. Go to that method in GameLayer.cpp and add the following code:

```
_jet = ParticleSystemQuad::create("jet.plist");
_jet->setSourcePosition(Vec2(-_rocket->getRadius() * 0.8f,0));
_jet->setAngle(180);
_jet->stopSystem();
this->addChild(_jet, kBackground);

_boom = ParticleSystemQuad::create("boom.plist");
_boom->stopSystem();
this->addChild(_boom, kForeground);

_comet = ParticleSystemQuad::create("comet.plist");
_comet->stopSystem();
_comet->setPosition(Vec2(0, _screenSize.height * 0.6f));
_comet->setVisible(false);
this->addChild(_comet, kForeground);

_pickup = ParticleSystemQuad::create("plink.plist");
_pickup->stopSystem();
this->addChild(_pickup, kMiddleground);
```

```
_warp = ParticleSystemQuad::create("warp.plist");
_warp->setPosition(_rocket->getPosition());
this->addChild(_warp, kBackground);

_star = ParticleSystemQuad::create("star.plist");
_star->stopSystem();
_star->setVisible(false);
this->addChild(_star, kBackground, kSpriteStar);
```

What just happened?

We created our first particles. ParticleDesigner exports the particle system data as a .plist file, which we used to create our ParticleSystemQuad objects. You should open one of these files in Xcode to review the number of settings used in a particle system. From Cocos2d-x you can modify any of these settings through setters inside ParticleSystem.

The particles we'll use in this game are as follows:

◆ _jet: This is attached to the _rocket object and it will trail behind the _rocket object. We set the system's angle and source position parameters to match the _rocket sprite.

◆ _boom: This is the particle system used when _rocket explodes.

◆ _comet: This is a particle system that moves across the screen at set intervals and can collide with _rocket.

◆ _pickup: This is used when a star is collected.

◆ _warp: This marks the initial position of the rocket.

◆ _star: This is the particle system used for the star that the rocket must collect.

The following screenshot shows these various particles:

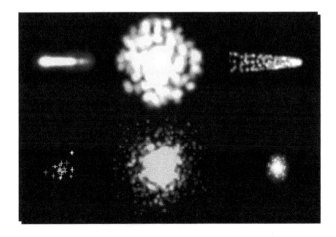

All particle systems are added as children to `GameLayer`; they cannot be added to our `SpriteBatchNode` class. And you must call `stopSystem()` on each system as they're created otherwise they will start playing as soon as they are added to a node.

In order to run the system, you make a call to `resetSystem()`.

 Cocos2d-x comes bundled with some common particle systems you can modify for your own needs. If you go to the `test` folder at: `tests/cpp-tests/Classes/ParticleTest`, you will see examples of these systems being used. The actual particle data files are found at: `tests/cpp-tests/Resources/Particles`.

Creating the grid

Let's take some time now to review the grid logic in the game. This grid is created inside the `createStarGrid` method in `GameLayer.cpp`. What the method does is determine all possible spots on the screen where we can place the `_star` particle system.

We use a C++ vector list called `_grid` to store the available spots:

```
std::vector<Point> _grid;
```

The `createStarGrid` method divides the screen into multiple cells of 32 x 32 pixels, ignoring the areas too close to the screen borders (`gridFrame`). Then we check the distance between each cell and the planet sprites stored inside the vector `_planets`. If the cell is far enough from the planets, we store it inside the `_grid` vector as `Point`.

In the following figure, you can get an idea of the result we're after. We want all the white cells not overlapping any of the planets.

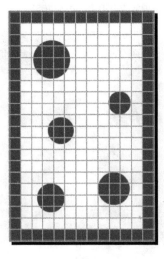

We output a message to the console with `Log` stating how many cells we end up with:

```
CCLOG("POSSIBLE STARS: %i", _grid.size());
```

This `vector` list will be shuffled at each new game, so we end up with a random sequence of possible positions for our star:

```
std::random_shuffle(_grid.begin(), _grid.end());
```

This way we never place a star on top of a planet or so close to it that the rocket could not reach it without colliding with the planet.

Drawing primitives in Cocos2d-x

One of the main elements in the game is the `LineContainer.cpp` class. It is a `DrawNode` derived class that allows us to draw lines and circles on the screen.

`DrawNode` comes bundled with a list of drawing methods you can use to draw lines, points, circles, polygons, and so on.

The methods we'll use are `drawLine` and `drawDot`.

Time for action – let's do some drawing!

Time to implement the drawing inside `LineContainer.cpp`. You will notice that this class already has most of its methods implemented, so you can save a little typing. I'll go over what these methods represent once we add the game's main update method. But basically `LineContainer` will be used to display the lines the player draws on screen to manipulate `_rocket` sprite, as well as display an energy bar that acts as a sort of timer in our game:

1. What we need to change here is the `update` method. So this is what you need to type inside that method:

    ```
    _energy -= dt * _energyDecrement;
    if (_energy < 0) _energy = 0;
    clear();

    switch (_lineType) {
      case LINE_NONE:
       break;
      case LINE_TEMP:
       drawLine(_tip, _pivot, Color4F(1.0, 1.0, 1.0, 1.0));
       drawDot(_pivot, 5, Color4F(Color3B::WHITE));
       break;
    ```

```
        case LINE_DASHED:
            drawDot(_pivot, 5, Color4F(Color3B::WHITE));
            int segments = _lineLength / (_dash + _dashSpace);
            float t = 0.0f;
            float x_;
            float y_;

            for (int i = 0; i < segments + 1; i++) {
                x_ = _pivot.x + t * (_tip.x - _pivot.x);
                y_ = _pivot.y + t * (_tip.y - _pivot.y);
                drawDot(Vec2(x_, y_), 5, Color4F(Color3B::WHITE));
                t += (float) 1 / segments;
            }
            break;
    }
```

2. We end our drawing calls by drawing the energy bar in the same
    `LineContainer` node:

```
    drawLine(Vec2(_energyLineX, _screenSize.height * 0.1f),
    Vec2(_energyLineX, _screenSize.height * 0.9f), Color4F(0.0, 0.0,
    0.0, 1.0));

    drawLine(Vec2(_energyLineX, _screenSize.height * 0.1f),
    Vec2(_energyLineX, _screenSize.height * 0.1f + _energy *
    _energyHeight ), Color4F(1.0, 0.5, 0.0, 1.0));
```

What just happened?

You just learned how to draw inside `DrawNode`. One important line in that code is the
`clear()` call. It clears all the drawings in that node before we update them with their
new state.

In `LineContainer`, we use a `switch` statement to determine how to draw the player's line.
If the `_lineType` property is set to `LINE_NONE`, we don't draw anything (this will, in effect,
clear the screen of any drawings done by the player).

If `_lineType` is `LINE_TEMP`, this means the player is currently dragging a finger away from
the `_rocket` object, and we want to show a white line from the `_rocket` current position
to the player's current touch position. These points are called `tip` and `pivot`, respectively.

We also draw a dot right on the `pivot` point.

```
    drawLine(_tip, _pivot, Color4F(1.0, 1.0, 1.0, 1.0));
    drawDot(_pivot, 5, Color4F(Color3B::WHITE));
```

If `_lineType` is `LINE_DASHED`, it means the player has removed his or her finger from the screen and set a new pivot point for the `_rocket` to rotate around. We draw a white dotted line, using what is known as the Bezier linear formula to draw a series of tiny circles from the `_rocket` current position and the `pivot` point:

```
for (int i = 0; i < segments + 1; i++) {

    x_ = _pivot.x + t * (_tip.x - _pivot.x);
    y_ = _pivot.y + t * (_tip.y - _pivot.y);

    drawDot(Vec2(x_, y_), 5, Color4F(Color3B::WHITE));
    t += (float) 1 / segments;
}
```

And finally, for the energy bar, we draw a black line underneath an orange one. The orange one resizes as the value for `_energy` in `LineContainer` is reduced. The black one stays the same and it's here to show contrast. You layer your drawings through the order of your `draw` calls; so the first things drawn appear underneath the latter ones.

The rocket sprite

Time to tackle the second object in the game: the rocket.

Once again, I already put in place the part of the logic that's old news to you. But please review the code already inside `Rocket.cpp`. We have a method to reset the rocket every time a new game starts (`reset`), and a method to show the selected state of the rocket (`select(bool flag)`) by changing its displayed texture:

```
if (flag) {
    this->setDisplayFrame(SpriteFrameCache::getInstance()-
>getSpriteFrameByName("rocket_on.png"));
} else {
    this->setDisplayFrame(SpriteFrameCache::getInstance()-
>getSpriteFrameByName("rocket.png"));
}
```

This will either show the rocket with a glow around it, or not.

And finally a method to check collision with the sides of the screen (`collidedWithSides`). If there is a collision, we adjust the rocket so it moves away from the screen side it collided with, and we release it from any pivot point.

What we really need to worry about here is the rocket's `update` method. And that's what we'll add next.

Time for action – updating our rocket sprite

The game's main loop will call the rocket's `update` method in every iteration.

1. Inside the empty `update` method in `Rocket.cpp`, add the following lines:

```
Point position = this->getPosition();
if (_rotationOrientation == ROTATE_NONE) {
  position.x += _vector.x * dt;
  position.y += _vector.y * dt;
} else {
  float angle = _angularSpeed * dt;
  Point rotatedPoint = position.rotateByAngle(_pivot, angle);
  position.x = rotatedPoint.x;
  position.y = rotatedPoint.y;
  float rotatedAngle;

  Point diff = position;
  diff.subtract(_pivot);
  Point clockwise = diff.getRPerp();

  if (_rotationOrientation == ROTATE_COUNTER) {
    rotatedAngle = atan2 (-1 * clockwise.y, -1 * clockwise.x);
  } else {
    rotatedAngle = atan2 (clockwise.y, clockwise.x);
  }

  _vector.x = _speed * cos (rotatedAngle);
  _vector.y = _speed * sin (rotatedAngle);
  this->setRotationFromVector();

  if (this->getRotation() > 0) {
    this->setRotation( fmodf(this->getRotation(), 360.0f) );
  } else {
    this->setRotation( fmodf(this->getRotation(), -360.0f) );
  }
}
```

2. Here we are saying, if the rocket is not rotating (`_rotationOrientation ==`
`ROTATE_NONE`), just move it according to its current `_vector`. If it is rotating, then
use the Cocos2d-x helper `rotateByAngle` method to find its next position around
its pivot point:

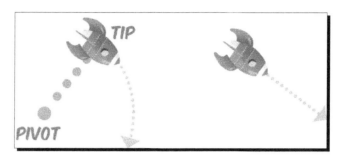

3. The method will rotate any point around a pivot by a certain angle. So we rotate
the rocket's updated position around its pivot (determined by the player) using a
property of `Rocket` class called `_angularSpeed`; we'll see in a moment how it
gets calculated.

4. Based on whether the rocket is rotating clockwise or counterclockwise, we adjust its
rotation so the rocket will be at a 90 degree angle with the line drawn between the
rocket and its pivot point. Then we change the rocket's movement vector based on
this rotated angle, and we wrap the value of that angle between 0 and 360.

5. Finish up the `update` method with these lines:

```
if (_targetRotation > this->getRotation() + 180) {
  _targetRotation -= 360;
}
if (_targetRotation < this->getRotation() - 180) {
  _targetRotation += 360;
}

this->setPosition(position);
_dr = _targetRotation - this->getRotation() ;
_ar = _dr * _rotationSpring;
_vr += _ar ;
_vr *= _rotationDamping;
float rotationNow = this->getRotation();
rotationNow += _vr;
this->setRotation(rotationNow);
```

6. With these lines we determine the new target rotation of our sprite and we run an
animation to rotate the rocket to its target rotation (with a bit of a spring to it).

What just happened?

We just wrote the logic that will move the rocket around the screen, whether the rocket is rotating or not.

So when the player picks a pivot point for the _rocket sprite, this pivot point is passed to both Rocket and LineContainer. The former will use it to rotate its vector around it and the latter will use it to draw a dotted line between _rocket and the pivot point.

> We can't use Action to rotate the sprite because the target rotation is updated too many times in our logic, and Action needs time to initialize and run.

So it's time to code the touch events to make all that logic fall into place.

Time for action – handling touches

We need to implement onTouchBegan, onTouchMoved, and onTouchEnded.

1. Now in GameLayer.cpp, inside onTouchBegan, add the following lines:

```
if (!_running) return true;

Point tap = touch->getLocation();
float dx = _rocket->getPositionX() - tap.x;
float dy = _rocket->getPositionY() - tap.y;
if (dx * dx + dy * dy <= pow(_rocket->getRadius(), 2) ) {
  _lineContainer->setLineType ( LINE_NONE );
  _rocket->setRotationOrientation ( ROTATE_NONE );
  _drawing = true;
}

return true;
```

When a touch begins, we only need to determine whether it's touching the ship. If it is, we set our _drawing property to true. This will indicate we have a valid point (one that began by touching the _rocket sprite).

2. We clear any lines we may be currently drawing in _lineContainer by calling setLineType(LINE_NONE), and we make sure _rocket will not rotate until we have a pivot point by releasing _rocket (setRotationOrientation (ROTATE_NONE)), so it will continue to move on its current linear trajectory (_vector).

3. From here, we begin drawing a new line with the next `onTouchMoved` method. Inside that method, we add the following lines:

```
if (!_running) return;
  if (_drawing) {
     Point tap = touch->getLocation();
     float dx = _rocket->getPositionX() - tap.x;
     float dy = _rocket->getPositionY() - tap.y;
     if (dx * dx + dy * dy > pow (_minLineLength, 2)) {
        _rocket->select(true);
        _lineContainer->setPivot ( tap );
        _lineContainer->setLineType ( LINE_TEMP );
     } else {
        _rocket->select(false);
        _lineContainer->setLineType ( LINE_NONE );
     }
  }
```

4. We'll handle touch moved only if we are using `_drawing`, which means the player has pressed on the ship and is now dragging his or her finger across the screen.

Once the distance between the finger and `_rocket` is greater than the `_minLineLength` distance we stipulate in game `init`, then we give a visual cue to the player by adding a glow around `_rocket` (`_rocket->select(true)`), and we draw the new line in `_lineContainer` by passing it the touch's current position and setting the line type to `LINE_TEMP`. If the minimum length is not reached, we don't show a line and nor do we show the player selected.

5. Next comes `onTouchEnded`. There is logic in place already inside our `onTouchEnded` method which deals with game states. You should uncomment the calls to `resetGame` and add a new `else if` statement inside the method:

```
} else if (_state == kGamePaused) {
   _pauseBtn->setDisplayFrame(SpriteFrameCache::getInstance()-
>getSpriteFrameByName ("btn_pause_off.png"));
   _paused->setVisible(false);
   _state = kGamePlay;
   _running = true;
   return;
}
```

6. If the game is paused, we change the texture in the `_pauseBtn` sprite through `Sprite->setDisplayFrame`, and we start running the game again.

7. Now we begin handling the touch. First, we determine whether it's landing on the Pause **button**:

```
if (!_running) return;
if(touch != nullptr) {
  Point tap = touch->getLocation();
  if (_pauseBtn->getBoundingBox().containsPoint(tap)) {
    _paused->setVisible(true);
    _state = kGamePaused;
    _pauseBtn->setDisplayFrame(SpriteFrameCache::getInstance()-
>getSpriteFrameByName ("btn_pause_on.png"));
    _running = false;
    return;
  }
}
```

8. If so, we change the game state to kGamePaused, change the texture on the _pauseBtn sprite (by retrieving another sprite frame from SpriteFrameCache), stop running the game (pausing it), and return from the function.

9. We can finally do something about the rocket ship. So, continuing inside the same if(touch != nullptr) { conditional seen previously, add these lines:

```
  _drawing = false;
  _rocket->select(false);
  if (_lineContainer->getLineType() == LINE_TEMP) {
    _lineContainer->setPivot (tap);
    _lineContainer->setLineLength ( _rocket->getPosition().
distance( tap ) );
    _rocket->setPivot (tap);
```

10. We start by deselecting the _rocket sprite, and then we check whether we are currently showing a temporary line in _lineContainer. If we are, this means we can go ahead and create our new pivot point with the player's released touch. We pass this information to _lineContainer with our setPivot method, along with the line length. The _rocket sprite also receives the pivot point information.

Then, things get hairy! The _rocket sprite is moving at a pixel-based speed. Once _rocket starts rotating, it will move at an angular-based speed through Point. rotateByAngle. So the following lines are added to translate the _rocket current pixel-based speed into angular speed:

```
float circle_length = _lineContainer->getLineLength() * 2 * M_PI;
int iterations = floor(circle_length / _rocket->getSpeed());
_rocket->setAngularSpeed ( 2 * M_PI / iterations);
```

11. It grabs the length of the circumference about to be described by `_rocket` (`line length * 2 * PI`) and divides it by the rocket's speed, getting in return the number of iterations needed for the rocket to complete that length. Then the 360 degrees of the circle is divided by the same number of iterations (but we do it in radians) to arrive at the fraction of the circle that the rocket must rotate at each iteration: its angular speed.

12. What follows next is even more math, using the amazingly helpful methods from Cocos2d-x related to vector math (`Point.getRPerp`, `Point.dot`, `Point.subtract`, to name a few) some of which we've seen already in the `Rocket` class:

```
Vec2 diff = _rocket->getPosition();
diff.subtract(_rocket->getPivot());
Point clockwise = diff.getRPerp();
float dot =clockwise.dot(_rocket->getVector());
if (dot > 0) {
    _rocket->setAngularSpeed ( _rocket->getAngularSpeed() * -1 );
    _rocket->setRotationOrientation ( ROTATE_CLOCKWISE );
    _rocket->setTargetRotation
( CC_RADIANS_TO_DEGREES( atan2(clockwise.y, clockwise.x) ) );
} else {
    _rocket->setRotationOrientation ( ROTATE_COUNTER );
    _rocket->setTargetRotation ( CC_RADIANS_TO_DEGREES
(atan2(-1 * clockwise.y, -1 * clockwise.x) ) );
}
_lineContainer->setLineType ( LINE_DASHED );
```

13. What they do here is determine which direction the rocket should rotate to: clockwise or counterclockwise, based on its current vector of movement.

14. The line the player just drew between `_rocket` and pivot point, which we get by subtracting (`Point.subtract`) those two points, has two perpendicular vectors: one to the right (clockwise) that you get through `Point.getRPerp` and one to the left (counterclockwise) that you get through `Point.getPerp`. We use the angle of one of these vectors as the `_rocket` target rotation so the rocket will rotate to be at 90 degrees with the line drawn in `LineContainer`. And we find the correct perpendicular through the dot product of the `_rocket` current vector and one of the perpendiculars (`Point.dot`).

What just happened?

I know. A lot of math and all at once! Thankfully, Cocos2d-x made it all much easier to handle.

We just added the logic that allows the player to draw lines and set new pivot points for the `_rocket` sprite.

The player will steer the _rocket sprite through the planets by giving the rocket a pivot point to rotate around. And by releasing the _rocket from pivot points, the player will make it move in a straight line again. All that logic gets managed here in the game's touch events.

And don't worry about the math. Though understanding how to deal with vectors is a very useful tool in any game developer's toolbox, and you should definitely research the topic, there are countless games you can still build with little or no math; so cheer up!

The game loop

It's time to create our good old ticker! The main loop will be in charge of collision detection, updating the points inside _lineContainer, adjusting our _jet particle system to our _rocket sprite, and a few other things.

Time for action – adding the main loop

Let's implement our main update method.

1. In GameLayer.cpp, inside the update method, add the following lines:

```
if (!_running || _state != kGamePlay) return;
if (_lineContainer->getLineType() != LINE_NONE) {
  _lineContainer->setTip (_rocket->getPosition() );
}

if (_rocket->collidedWithSides()) {
  _lineContainer->setLineType ( LINE_NONE );
}
_rocket->update(dt);

//update jet particle so it follows rocket
if (!_jet->isActive()) _jet->resetSystem();
_jet->setRotation(_rocket->getRotation());
_jet->setPosition(_rocket->getPosition());
```

We check to see if we are not currently on pause. Then, if there is a line for our ship that we need to show in _lineContainer, we update the line's tip point with the _rocket current position.

We run collision checks between _rocket and the screen sides, update the _rocket sprite, and position and rotate our _jet particle system to align it with the _rocket sprite.

2. Next we update _comet (its countdown, initial position, movement, and collision with _rocket if _comet is visible):

```
_cometTimer += dt;
float newY;

if (_cometTimer > _cometInterval) {
    _cometTimer = 0;
    if (_comet->isVisible() == false) {
        _comet->setPositionX(0);
        newY =
        (float)rand()/((float)RAND_MAX/_screenSize.height *
        0.6f) + _screenSize.height * 0.2f;
        if (newY > _screenSize.height * 0.9f)
            newY = _screenSize.height * 0.9f;
        _comet->setPositionY(newY);
        _comet->setVisible(true);
        _comet->resetSystem();
    }
}

if (_comet->isVisible()) {
    //collision with comet
    if (pow(_comet->getPositionX() - _rocket->getPositionX(),
    2) + pow(_comet->getPositionY() - _rocket->getPositionY(),
    2) <= pow (_rocket->getRadius() , 2)) {
        if (_rocket->isVisible()) killPlayer();
    }
    _comet->setPositionX(_comet->getPositionX() + 50 * dt);

    if (_comet->getPositionX() > _screenSize.width * 1.5f) {
        _comet->stopSystem();
        _comet->setVisible(false);
    }
}
```

3. Next we update _lineContainer, and slowly reduce the opacity of the _rocket sprite based on the _energy level in _lineContainer:

```
_lineContainer->update(dt);
_rocket->setOpacity(_lineContainer->getEnergy() * 255);
```

This will add a visual cue for the player that time is running out as the _rocket sprite will slowly turn invisible.

4. Run collision with planets:

```
for (auto planet : _planets) {
    if (pow(planet->getPositionX() - _rocket->getPositionX(),
    2)
    + pow(planet->getPositionY() - _rocket->getPositionY(), 2)
    <=   pow (_rocket->getRadius() * 0.8f + planet->getRadius()
    * 0.65f, 2)) {

        if (_rocket->isVisible()) killPlayer();
        break;
    }
}
```

5. And collision with the star:

```
if (pow(_star->getPositionX() - _rocket->getPositionX(), 2)
    + pow(_star->getPositionY() - _rocket->getPositionY(), 2)
    <=
    pow (_rocket->getRadius() * 1.2f, 2)) {

    _pickup->setPosition(_star->getPosition());
    _pickup->resetSystem();
    if (_lineContainer->getEnergy() + 0.25f < 1) {
        _lineContainer->setEnergy(_lineContainer->getEnergy() +
        0.25f);
    } else {
        _lineContainer->setEnergy(1.0);
    }
    _rocket->setSpeed(_rocket->getSpeed() + 2);
    if (_rocket->getSpeed() > 70) _rocket->setSpeed(70);
        _lineContainer->setEnergyDecrement(0.0002f);
        SimpleAudioEngine::getInstance()->playEffect("pickup.
wav");
        resetStar();

        int points = 100 - _timeBetweenPickups;
        if (points < 0) points = 0;

        _score += points;
        _scoreDisplay->setString(String::createWithFormat("%i",
_score)->getCString());
        _timeBetweenPickups = 0;
}
```

When we collect _star, we activate the _pickup particle system on the spot where _star was, we fill up the player's energy level, we make the game slightly harder, and we immediately reset _star to its next position to be collected again.

The score is based on the time it took the player to collect _star.

6. And we keep track of this time on the last lines of `update` where we also check the energy level:

```
_timeBetweenPickups += dt;
if (_lineContainer->getEnergy() == 0) {
    if (_rocket->isVisible()) killPlayer();
}
```

What just happened?

We added the main loop to our game and finally have all the pieces talking to each other. But you probably noticed quite a few calls to methods we have not implemented yet, such as `killPlayer` and `resetStar`. We'll finish our game logic with these methods.

Kill and reset

It's that time again! Time to kill our player and reset the game! We also need to move the `_star` sprite to a new position whenever it's picked up by the player.

Time for action – adding our resets and kills

We need to add logic to restart our game and to move our pickup star to a new position. But first, let's kill the player!

1. Inside the `killPlayer` method, add the following lines:

```
void GameLayer::killPlayer() {

    SimpleAudioEngine::getInstance()->stopBackgroundMusic();
    SimpleAudioEngine::getInstance()->stopAllEffects();
    SimpleAudioEngine::getInstance()->playEffect("shipBoom.wav");

    _boom->setPosition(_rocket->getPosition());
    _boom->resetSystem();
    _rocket->setVisible(false);
    _jet->stopSystem();
    _lineContainer->setLineType ( LINE_NONE );

    _running = false;
    _state = kGameOver;
    _gameOver->setVisible(true);
    _pauseBtn->setVisible(false);
}
```

2. Inside `resetStar`, add the following lines:

```
void GameLayer::resetStar() {
    Point position = _grid[_gridIndex];
    _gridIndex++;
    if (_gridIndex == _grid.size()) _gridIndex = 0;
    //reset star particles
    _star->setPosition(position);
    _star->setVisible(true);
    _star->resetSystem();
}
```

3. And finally, our `resetGame` method:

```
void GameLayer::resetGame () {

    _rocket->setPosition(Vec2(_screenSize.width * 0.5f,
    _screenSize.height * 0.1f));
    _rocket->setOpacity(255);
    _rocket->setVisible(true);
    _rocket->reset();

    _cometInterval = 4;
    _cometTimer = 0;
    _timeBetweenPickups = 0.0;

    _score = 0;
    _scoreDisplay->setString(String::createWithFormat("%i", _
    score)->getCString());

    _lineContainer->reset();

    //shuffle grid cells

    std::random_shuffle(_grid.begin(), _grid.end());
    _gridIndex = 0;

    resetStar();

    _warp->stopSystem();

    _running = true;

    SimpleAudioEngine::getInstance()->playBackgroundMusic("backgro
und.mp3", true);
    SimpleAudioEngine::getInstance()->stopAllEffects();
    SimpleAudioEngine::getInstance()->playEffect("rocket.wav",
true);

}
```

What just happened?

That's it. We're done. It took more math than most people are comfortable with. But what can I tell you, I just love messing around with vectors!

Now, let's move on to Android!

Time for action – running the game in Android

Follow these steps to deploy the game to Android:

1. Open the manifest file and set the app orientation to portrait.

2. Next, open the Android.mk file in a text editor.

3. Edit the lines in LOCAL_SRC_FILES to read:

```
LOCAL_SRC_FILES := hellocpp/main.cpp \
                   ../../Classes/AppDelegate.cpp \
                   ../../Classes/GameSprite.cpp \
                   ../../Classes/LineContainer.cpp \
                   ../../Classes/Rocket.cpp \
                   ../../Classes/GameLayer.cpp
```

4. Import the game into Eclipse and build it.

5. Save and run your application. This time, you can try out different size screens if you have the devices.

What just happened?

You now have Rocket Through running in Android.

Have a go hero

Add logic to the resetStar method so that the new position picked is not too close to the _rocket sprite. So, make the function a recurrent one until a proper position is picked.

And take the warp particle system, which right now does not do a whole lot, and use it as a random teleport field so that the rocket may get sucked in by a randomly placed warp and moved farther away from the target star.

Summary

Congratulations! You now have enough information about Cocos2d-x to produce awesome 2D games. First sprites, then actions, and now particles.

Particles make everything look shiny! They are easy to implement and are a very good way to add an extra bit of animation to your game. But it's very easy to overdo it, so be careful. You don't want to give your players epileptic fits. Also, running too many particles at once could stop your game in its tracks.

In the next chapter, we'll see how to use Cocos2d-x to quickly test and develop game ideas.

6
Quick and Easy Sprite – Victorian Rush Hour

In our fourth example of a game built with Cocos2d-x, I'll show you a simple technique for rapid prototyping. Often in game development, you want to test the core ideas of your game as soon as possible, because a game may sound fun in your head but in reality it just doesn't work. Rapid prototyping techniques allow you to test your game as early as possible in the development process as well as build up on the good ideas.

Here's what you'll learn:

- ◆ How to quickly create placeholder sprites
- ◆ How to code collisions for a platform game
- ◆ How to create varied terrain for a side-scroller

The game – Victorian Rush Hour

In this game (Victorian Rush Hour), you control a cyclist in Victorian London trying to avoid rush-hour traffic on his way home. For reasons no one can explain, he's riding his bike on top of the buildings. As the player, it is your job to ensure he makes it.

The controls are very simple: you tap the screen to make the cyclist jump and while he's in the air, if you tap the screen again, the cyclist will open his trusty umbrella, either slowing his descent or adding a boost to his jump.

This game is of a type commonly known as a dash game or endless runner, a genre that has become increasingly popular online and on various app stores. Usually in these types of games you, the developer, have two choices: either make the terrain the main obstacle and challenge in the game, or make what's added to the terrain the main challenge (enemies, pick-ups, obstacles, and so on). With this game, I decided on the first option.

So our challenge is to create a game where the terrain is the enemy but not an unbeatable one.

The game settings

The game is a universal application, designed for the iPad retina display but with support for other display sizes. It is played in the landscape mode and it does not support multitouch.

Rapid prototyping with Cocos2d-x

The idea behind this is to create sprites as placeholders for your game elements as quickly as possible, so you can test your game ideas and refine them. Every game in this book was initially developed in the way I'm about to show you, with simple rectangles in place of textured sprites.

The technique shown here allows you to create rectangles of any size and of any color to be used in your game logic:

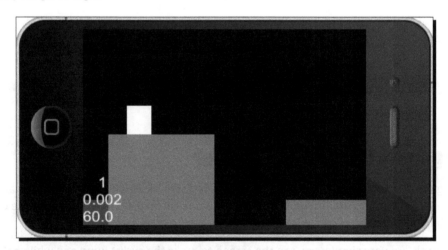

Time for action – creating placeholder sprites

So let me show you how to do that:

1. Go ahead and download the `4198_06_START_PROJECT.zip` file if you haven't done so already.

2. When you open the project in Xcode, you will see all the classes we'll need for the game, and we'll go over them in a second. But for now, just go to `GameLayer.cpp`.

3. Scroll down to the last `createGameScreen` method and add the following lines:

```
auto quickSprite = Sprite::create("blank.png");
quickSprite->setTextureRect(Rect(0, 0, 100, 100));
quickSprite->setColor(Color3B(255,255,255));

quickSprite->setPosition(Vec2(_screenSize.width * 0.5, _
screenSize.height * 0.5));
this->addChild(quickSprite);
```

And that's it. The sprite is created with a texture called `blank.png`. This is a 1 x 1 pixel white square you will find in the `Resources` folder. Then we set the size of the sprite's texture rectangle to 100 x 100 pixels (`setTextureRect`), and fill it with a white color (`setColor`). By resizing the texture rectangle, we in effect resize the sprite. If you run the game now, you should see a white square smack in the middle of the screen.

4. Now delete the previous lines and replace them with these:

```
_gameBatchNode = SpriteBatchNode::create("blank.png", 200);
this->addChild(_gameBatchNode, kMiddleground);
```

This creates `_gameBatchNode` that uses as its source texture the same `blank.png` file. Now we are ready to place as many rectangles inside `_gameBatchNode` as we'd like, and set a different color for each one of them if we want. We can, in other words, build an entire test game with one tiny image. Which is what we'll proceed to do now.

5. So, to finish up here, add these last lines:

```
_terrain = Terrain::create();
_gameBatchNode->addChild(_terrain, kMiddleground);

_player = Player::create();
_gameBatchNode->addChild(_player, kBackground);
```

What just happened?

We just created a placeholder sprite we can use to test gameplay ideas quickly and painlessly. And we created our game's two main objects: the `Player` and `Terrain` object. These are empty shells at the moment, but we'll start working on them next. But first let's go over the different game elements.

The Player object

This represents our cyclist. It will jump, float, and collide with the `_terrain` object. Its x speed is passed to the `_terrain` object causing the `Terrain` object to move, side scrolling to the left of the screen.

The `Player` object derives, once again, from a `GameSprite` class. This one has getters and setters for next position, vector of movement, and the sprite's width and height.

The `Player` interface has inline helper methods to retrieve information about its rectangle boundaries related to its current position (left, right, top, bottom), and its next position (`next_left`, `next_right`, `next_top`, `next_bottom`). These will be used in collision detection with the `_terrain` object.

The Block object

These objects form the individual pieces of the `_terrain` object. They can take the shape of a building, or an empty gap between buildings. We'll have four different types of buildings, which later will represent four different types of textures when we finally bring in our sprite sheets. These blocks can have different widths and heights.

`Block` also derives from `GameSprite` and it also has inline helper methods to retrieve information about its boundaries, but only in relation to its current position, since `Block` doesn't technically move.

The terrain object

This object contains the individual `Block` objects that form the landscape. It contains just enough `Block` objects to fill the screen, and as the `_terrain` object scrolls to the left, the `Block` objects that leave the screen are moved to the far right side of the `_terrain` and reused as new blocks, ensuring continuous scrolling.

The _terrain object is also responsible for collision checks with the _player object, since it has quick access to all information we'll need for collision detection; namely the list of blocks currently on the screen, their size, type, and position. Our main loop then will call on the Terrain object to test for collision with the player object.

Let's work on these main objects, starting with the Player object.

Time for action – coding the player

Open up the Player.cpp class.

1. The _player object is created through a static method that uses our blank.png file to texture the sprite. That method also makes a call to initPlayer, and this is what you should type for that method:

```
void Player::initPlayer () {
    this->setAnchorPoint(Vec2(0.5f, 1.0f));
    this->setPosition(Vec2(_screenSize.width * 0.2f, _
nextPosition.y));

    _height = 228;
    _width = 180;
    this->setTextureRect(Rect(0, 0, _width, _height));
    this->setColor(Color3B(255,255,255));
}
```

The _player object will have its registration point at the top of the sprite. The reason behind this top center anchor point has much more to do with the way the _player object will be animated when floating, than with any collision logic requirements.

2. Next comes setFloating:

```
void Player::setFloating (bool value) {

    if (_floating == value) return;

    if (value && _hasFloated) return;

    _floating = value;

    if (value) {
        _hasFloated = true;
        _vector.y += PLAYER_JUMP * 0.5f;
    }
}
```

The `_hasFloated` property will ensure the player can only open the umbrella once while in the air. And when we set `_floating` to `true`, we give the `_player.y` vector a boost.

3. We begin the update method of `_player` with:

```
void Player::update (float dt) {
    if (_speed + P_ACCELERATION <= _maxSpeed) {
        _speed += P_ACCELERATION;
    } else {
        _speed = _maxSpeed;
    }

    _vector.x = _speed;
```

The game will increase `_maxSpeed` of the `_player` object as time goes on, making the game more difficult. These first lines make the change from the `_players` current `_speed` up to `_maxSpeed` a bit smoother and not an immediate change.

Victorian Rush Hour has no levels, so it's important to figure out a way to make it incrementally harder to play, and yet not impossible. Finding that sweet spot in your logic may take some time and it's one more reason to test game ideas as soon as possible. Here we make the game harder by increasing the player's speed and the size of the gaps between buildings. These are updated inside a countdown in the main loop.

4. Next, we update the `_player` object based on its `_state` of movement:

```
switch (_state) {

    case kPlayerMoving:
        _vector.y -= FORCE_GRAVITY;
        if (_hasFloated) _hasFloated = false;
        break;

    case kPlayerFalling:
        if (_floating ) {
            _vector.y -= FLOATNG_GRAVITY;
            _vector.x *= FLOATING_FRICTION;

        } else {
            _vector.y -= FORCE_GRAVITY;
            _vector.x *= AIR_FRICTION;
            _floatingTimer = 0;
        }
        break;

    case kPlayerDying:
```

```
    _vector.y -= FORCE_GRAVITY;
    _vector.x = - _speed;
    this->setPositionX(this->getPositionX() + _vector.x);
    break;

}
```

We have different values for gravity and friction depending on move state.

We also have a time limit for how long the _player object can be floating, and we reset that timer when the _player object is not floating. If the _player object is dying (collided with a wall), we move the _player object backward and downward until it leaves the screen.

5. We finish with:

```
if (_jumping) {
    _state = kPlayerFalling;
    _vector.y += PLAYER_JUMP * 0.25f;
    if (_vector.y > PLAYER_JUMP ) _jumping = false;
}

if (_vector.y < -TERMINAL_VELOCITY)
    _vector.y = -TERMINAL_VELOCITY;

_nextPosition.y = this->getPositionY() + _vector.y;

if (_floating) {
    _floatingTimer += dt;
    if (_floatingTimer > _floatingTimerMax) {
        _floatingTimer = 0;
        this->setFloating(false);
    }
}
}
```

When the player presses the screen for a jump, we shouldn't make the sprite jump immediately. Changes in state should always happen smoothly. So we have a boolean property in _player called _jumping. It is set to true when the player presses the screen and we slowly add the jump force to _vector.y. So the longer the player presses the screen, the higher the jump will be and a quick tap will result in a shorter jump. This is a nice feature to add to any platform game.

We next limit the y speed with a terminal velocity, update the next position of the _player object, and update the floating timer if _player is floating.

What just happened?

The `_player` object is updated through a series of states. Touching the screen will make changes to this `_state` property, as will the results of collision checking with `_terrain`.

Now let's work on the `Block` class.

Time for action – coding the Block object

Once again a static method, `create`, will use `blank.png` to create our `Block` sprite. Only this time, we don't actually change the texture rectangle for `Block` inside `create`:

1. The `Block` object is properly textured inside the `setupBlock` method:

```
void Block::setupBlock (int width, int height, int type) {

    _type = type;

    _width = width * _tileWidth;
    _height = height * _tileHeight;

    this->setAnchorPoint(Vec2(0,0));
    this->setTextureRect(Rect(0, 0, _width, _height));
```

A `Block` object's appearance will be based on its type, width, and height.

The `Block` sprite's registration point is set to top left. And we finally change the `Block` object's texture rectangle size here.

2. Then we set the `Block` object's color based on type:

```
switch (type) {

    case kBlockGap:
        this->setVisible(false);
        return;

    case kBlock1:

        this->setColor(Color3B(200,200,200));
        break;
    case kBlock2:

        this->setColor(Color3B(150,150,150));
        break;
```

```
        case kBlock3:

            this->setColor(Color3B(100,100,100));
            break;
        case kBlock4:

            this->setColor(Color3B(50,50,50));
        break;
    }

    this->setVisible(true);

}
```

kBlockGap means there is no building, just a gap the _player object must jump. We make the block invisible in that case and return from the function. So again, gaps are actually types of blocks in our logic.

In this test version, the different types of buildings are represented with different colors. Later we'll use different textures.

What just happened?

The Block object is very simple. We just need its values for _width and _height whether it's a gap or not, so we can properly run collision detection with these objects.

Planning the Terrain class

Before we jump to coding the Terrain class, we need to discuss a few things regarding randomness.

It is a very common mistake among game developers to confuse randomness with variableness, and very important to know when you need what.

A random number can be anything. 1234 is a random series of numbers. And the next time you want a random series of numbers and you once again get 1234 this will be just as random as the previous one. But not varied.

If you decide to build a random terrain, you will probably be disappointed in the result as it won't necessarily be varied. Also, remember that we need to make the terrain the key challenge of the game; but this means it can be neither too easy nor too difficult. True randomness would not allow us enough control here, or worse, we would end up with a long list of conditionals to make sure we have the correct combination of blocks, and that would result in at least one recurrent function inside our main loop, which is not a good idea.

We need instead to control the results and their variableness by applying our own patterns to them.

So we'll apply this logic of patterns to our _terrain object, forming a kind of pool of proper random choices. We'll use four arrays to store possible results in our decision making, and we'll shuffle three of these arrays during the game to add the "randomness" feel to our terrain.

These arrays are:

```
int patterns[] = {1,1,1,1,2,2,2,2,2,2,2,2,2,2,2,3,3,3};
```

This holds the information of how many buildings (Blocks) we have in a row, between gaps.

You can easily change the patterns value just by adding new values or by increasing or reducing the number of times one value appears. So here we're making a terrain with far more groupings of two buildings between gaps, than groups of three or one.

Next, consider the following lines:

```
int widths[] = {2,2,2,2,2,3,3,3,3,3,3,4,4,4,4,4,4};
int heights[] =
{0,0,0,0,0,0,0,0,0,0,1,1,1,1,1,1,1,2,2,2,3,3,3,3,3,3,4};
```

The preceding lines specify the widths and heights of each new building. These will be multiplied with the tile size determined for our game to get the final width and height values as you saw in Block:setupBlock.

We'll use a 0 value for height to mean there is no change in height from the previous building. A similar logic could be easily applied to widths.

And finally:

```
int types[] =
{1,2,3,4,1,3,2,4,3,2,1,4,2,3,1,4,2,3,1,2,3,2,3,4,1,2,4,3,1,3,1,4,2,4,
2,1,2,3};
```

These are building types and this array will not be shuffled unlike the three previous ones, so this is the patterns array of types we'll use throughout the game and it will loop continuously. You can make it as long as you wish.

Building the terrain object

So every time we need to create a new block, we'll set it up based on the information contained in these arrays.

This gives us far more control over the terrain, so that we don't create impossible combinations of obstacles for the player: a common mistake in randomly-built terrain for dash games.

But at the same time, we can easily expand this logic to fit every possible need. For instance, we could apply level logic to our game by creating multiple versions of these arrays, so as the game gets harder, we begin sampling data from arrays that contain particularly hard combinations of values.

And we can still use a conditional loop to refine results even further and I'll give you at least one example of this.

The values you saw in the `patterns` arrays will be stored inside the lists called `_blockPattern`, `_blockWidths`, `_blockHeights`, and `_blockTypes`.

The `Terrain` class then takes care of building the game's terrain in three stages. First we initialize the `_terrain` object, creating among other things a pool for `Block` objects. Then we add the first blocks to the `_terrain` object until a minimum width is reached to ensure the whole screen is populated with `Block`s. And finally we distribute the various block objects.

Time for action – initializing our Terrain class

We'll go over these steps next:

1. The first important method to implement is `initTerrain`:

    ```
    void Terrain::initTerrain () {

        _increaseGapInterval = 5000;
        _increaseGapTimer = 0;
        _gapSize = 2;

        //init object pools
        for (int i = 0; i < 20; i++) {
            auto block = Block::create();
            this->addChild(block);
            _blockPool.pushBack(block);
        }
    ```

```
_minTerrainWidth = _screenSize.width * 1.5f;

random_shuffle(_blockPattern.begin(), _blockPattern.end());
random_shuffle(_blockWidths.begin(), _blockWidths.end());
random_shuffle(_blockHeights.begin(), _blockHeights.end());

this->addBlocks(0);
}
```

We have a timer to increase the width of gaps (we begin with gaps two tiles long).

We create a pool for blocks so we don't instantiate any during the game. And 20 blocks is more than enough for what we need.

The blocks we are currently using in the terrain will be stored inside a `_blocks` vector.

We determine that the minimum width the `_terrain` object must have is `1.5` times the screen width. We'll keep adding blocks until the `_terrain` object reaches this minimum width. We end by shuffling the `patterns` arrays and adding the blocks.

2. The `addBlocks` method should look like this:

```
void Terrain::addBlocks(int currentWidth) {

    while (currentWidth < _minTerrainWidth)
    {
        auto block = _blockPool.at(_blockPoolIndex);
        _blockPoolIndex++;
        if (_blockPoolIndex == _blockPool.size()) {
          _blockPoolIndex = 0;
        }
        this->initBlock(block);
        currentWidth += block->getWidth();
        _blocks.pushBack(block);
    }
    this->distributeBlocks();
}
```

The logic inside the `while` loop will continue to add blocks until `currentWidth` of the `_terrain` object reaches `_minTerrainWidth`. Every new block we retrieve from the pool in order to reach `_minTerrainWidth` gets added to the `_blocks` vector.

3. Blocks are distributed based on their widths:

```
void Terrain::distributeBlocks() {
    int count = (int) _blocks.size();
    int i;

    for (i = 0; i < count; i++) {
        auto block = _blocks.at(i);
        if (i != 0) {
            auto prev_block = _blocks.at(i - 1);
            block->setPositionX( prev_block->getPositionX() + prev_
block->getWidth());
        }
        else
        {
            block->setPositionX ( 0 );
        }
    }
}
```

What just happened?

Terrain is a container of Blocks, and we just added the logic that will add a new block object to this container. Inside addBlocks, we call an initBlock method, which will use the information from our patterns arrays to initialize each block used in the terrain. It is this method we'll implement next.

Time for action – initializing our Blocks object

Finally, we will discuss the method that initializes the blocks based on our patterns array:

1. So inside the Terrain class, we start the initBlock method as follows:

```
void Terrain::initBlock(Block * block) {

    int blockWidth;
    int blockHeight;

    int type = _blockTypes[_currentTypeIndex];
    _currentTypeIndex++;

    if (_currentTypeIndex == _blockTypes.size()) {
        _currentTypeIndex = 0;
    }
```

Begin by determining the type of building we are initializing. See how we loop through the _blockTypes array using the index stored in _currentTypeIndex. We'll use a similar logic for the other patterns arrays.

2. Then, let's start building our blocks:

```
if (_startTerrain) {
    //...
} else {
    _lastBlockHeight = 2;
    _lastBlockWidth = rand() % 2 + 2;
    block->setupBlock (_lastBlockWidth, _lastBlockHeight, type);
}
```

The player must tap the screen to begin the game (_startTerrain). Until then, we show buildings with the same height (two tiles) and random width:

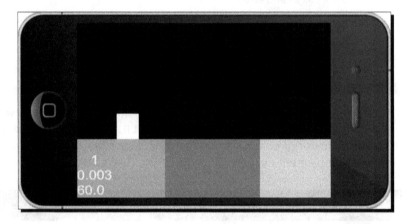

We will store _lastBlockHeight and _lastBlockWidth because the more information we have about the terrain the better we can apply our own conditions to it, as you will see in a moment.

3. Consider that we are set to _startTerrain:

```
if (_startTerrain) {
    if (_showGap) {
        int gap = rand() % _gapSize;
        if (gap < 2) gap = 2;

        block->setupBlock (gap, 0, kBlockGap);
        _showGap = false;
    } else {
        //...
```

In the following screenshot, you can see the different widths used for our blocks:

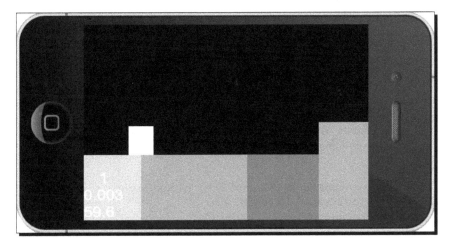

The information inside `_blockPattern` determines how many buildings we show in a row, and once a series is completed, we show a gap by setting the `boolean` value of `_showGap` to `true`. A gap's width is based on the current value of `_gapSize`, which may increase as the game gets harder and it can't be less than two times the tile width.

4. If we are not creating a gap this time, we determine the width and height of the new block based on the current indexed values of `_blockWidths` and `_blockHeights`:

```
} else {

    blockWidth = _blockWidths[_currentWidthIndex];

    _currentWidthIndex++;
    if (_currentWidthIndex == _blockWidths.size()) {
        random_shuffle(_blockWidths.begin(),
        _blockWidths.end());
        _currentWidthIndex = 0;
    }

    if (_blockHeights[_currentHeightIndex] != 0) {

        //change height of next block
        blockHeight = _blockHeights[_currentHeightIndex];
        //if difference too high, decrease it
        if (blockHeight - _lastBlockHeight > 2 && _gapSize ==
        2)
```

```
            {
                blockHeight = 1;
            }

        } else {
            blockHeight = _lastBlockHeight;
        }
        _currentHeightIndex++;
        if (_currentHeightIndex == _blockHeights.size()) {
            _currentHeightIndex = 0;
            random_shuffle(_blockHeights.begin(),
            _blockHeights.end());
        }

        block->setupBlock (blockWidth, blockHeight, type);
        _lastBlockWidth = blockWidth;
        _lastBlockHeight = blockHeight;
```

Notice how we reshuffle the arrays once we are done iterating through them (random_shuffle).

We use _lastBlockHeight to apply an extra condition to our terrain. We don't want the next block to be too tall in relation to the previous building, at least not in the beginning of the game, which we can determine by checking the value for _gapSize, which is only increased when the game gets harder.

And if the value from _blockHeights is 0, we don't change the height of the new building and use instead the same value from _lastBlockHeight.

5. We finish by updating the count in the current series of buildings to determine whether we should show a gap next, or not:

```
//select next block series pattern
_currentPatternCnt++;

if (_currentPatternCnt > _blockPattern[_currentPatternIndex]) {
    _showGap = true;
    //start new pattern
    _currentPatternIndex++;
    if (_currentPatternIndex == _blockPattern.size()) {
        random_shuffle(_blockPattern.begin(),
        _blockPattern.end());
        _currentPatternIndex = 0;
    }
    _currentPatternCnt = 1;
    }
}
```

What just happened?

We finally got to use our `patterns` arrays and build the blocks inside the terrain. The possibilities are endless here in how much control we can have in building our blocks. But the key idea here is to make sure the game does not become ridiculously hard, and I advise you to play some more with the values to achieve even better results (don't take my choices for granted).

Before we tackle collision, let's add the logic to move and reset the terrain.

Time for action – moving and resetting

We move the terrain inside the `move` method.

1. The `move` method receives as a parameter the amount of movement in the x axis:

```
void Terrain::move (float xMove) {
    if (xMove < 0) return;

    if (_startTerrain) {

        if (xMove > 0 && _gapSize < 5)
            _increaseGapTimer += xMove;

        if (_increaseGapTimer > _increaseGapInterval) {
            _increaseGapTimer = 0;
            _gapSize += 1;
        }
    }

    this->setPositionX(this->getPositionX() - xMove);

    auto  block = _blocks.at(0);
    if (_position.x + block->getWidth() < 0) {
        auto firstBlock = _blocks.at(0);
        _blocks.erase(0);
        _blocks.pushBack(firstBlock);
        _position.x +=  block->getWidth();

        float width_cnt = this->getWidth() - block->getWidth() - (
_blocks.at(0))->getWidth();
        this->initBlock(block);
        this->addBlocks(width_cnt);
    }
}
```

The value for xMove comes from the _player speed.

We start by updating the timer that will make the gaps wider. Then we move the terrain to the left. If after moving the terrain, a block leaves the screen, we move the block back to the end of the _blocks vector and reinitialize it as a new block through initBlock.

We make a call to addBlocks just in case the reinitialized block made the total width of the terrain less than the minimum width required.

2. Next, our reset method:

```
void Terrain::reset() {

    this->setPosition(Vec2(0,0));
    _startTerrain = false;

    int currentWidth = 0;
    for (auto block : _blocks) {
        this->initBlock(block);
        currentWidth +=  block->getWidth();
    }

    while (currentWidth < _minTerrainWidth) {
        auto block = _blockPool.at(_blockPoolIndex);
        _blockPoolIndex++;
        if (_blockPoolIndex == _blockPool.size()) {
            _blockPoolIndex = 0;
        }
        _blocks.pushBack(block);
        this->initBlock(block);
        currentWidth +=  block->getWidth();
    }

    this->distributeBlocks();
    _increaseGapTimer = 0;
    _gapSize = 2;
}
```

The reset method is called whenever we restart the game. We move _terrain back to its starting point, and we reinitialize all the current Block objects currently inside the _terrain object. This is done because we are back to _startTerrain = false, which means all blocks should have the same height and a random width.

If at the end of the reset we need more blocks to reach _minTerrainWidth, we add them accordingly.

What just happened?

We can now move the _terrain object and all the blocks it contains, and we can restart the process all over again if we need to.

Once again, using the container behavior of nodes simplified our job tremendously. When you scroll the terrain, you scroll all the Block objects it contains.

So we are finally ready to run collision logic.

Platform collision logic

We have in place all the information we need to check for collision through the inline methods found in Player and Block.

In this game, we'll need to check collision between the _player object's bottom side and the block object's top side, and between the _player object's right side and the Block class' left side. And we'll do that by checking the _player object's current position and its next position. We are looking for these conditions:

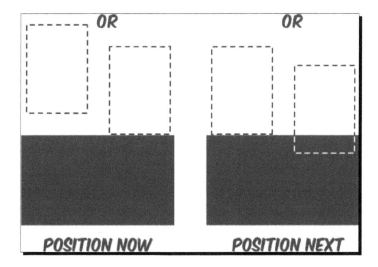

The diagram represents the conditions for bottom side collision, but the same idea applies to right side collision.

In the current position, the _player object must be above the top of the block or touching it. In the next position, the _player object must be either touching the top of the block or already overlapping it (or has moved past it altogether). This would mean a collision has occurred.

Time for action – adding collision detection

Let's see how that translates to code:

1. Still in `Terrain.cpp`:

```
void Terrain::checkCollision (Player * player) {

    if (player->getState() == kPlayerDying) return;
    bool inAir = true;
    for (auto block : _blocks) {
        if (block->getType() == kBlockGap) continue;

        //if within x, check y (bottom collision)
        if (player->right() >= this->getPositionX() + block->left()
&& player->left() <= this->getPositionX() + block->right()) {

            if (player->bottom() >= block->top() && player->next_
bottom() <= block->top() && player->top() > block->top()) {
                player->setNextPosition(Vec2(player-
>getNextPosition().x, block->top() + player->getHeight()));
                player->setVector ( Vec2(player->getVector().x, 0) );
                player->setRotation(0.0);
                inAir = false;
                break;
            }
        }
    }
```

First we state that the _player object is currently falling with `inAir = true`; we'll let the collision check determine if this will remain true or not.

We don't check the collision if _player is dying and we skip collision checks with any gap blocks.

We check collision on the y axis, which here means the bottom of the _player and top of the block. We first need to determine if the _player object is within range of the block we want to check against collision. This means the center of the _player object must be between the left and right side of the block; otherwise, the block is too far from the _player object and may be ignored.

Then we run a basic check to see if there is a collision between the _player object's current position and next position, using the conditions I explained earlier. If so, we fix the _player object's position and change its y vector speed to 0 and we determine that `inAir = false` after all, the _player object has landed.

2. Next we check collision on the x axis, meaning the right side of the `_player` object with the left side of the blocks:

```
for (auto block : _blocks) {
  if (block->getType() == kBlockGap) continue;
  //now if within y, check x (side collision)
  if ((player->bottom() < block->top() && player->top() >
block->bottom()) || (player->next_bottom() < block->top() &&
player->next_top() > block->bottom())) {
    if (player->right() >= this->getPositionX() + block-
>getPositionX()
&& player->left() < this->getPositionX() + block->getPositionX())
{
      player->setPositionX( this->getPositionX() +
block->getPositionX() - player->getWidth() * 0.5f );
      player->setNextPosition(Vec2(this->getPositionX() +
block->getPositionX() - player->getWidth() * 0.5f,
player->getNextPosition().y));
      player->setVector ( Vec2(player->getVector().x * -0.5f,
player->getVector().y) );
      if (player->bottom() + player->getHeight() * 0.2f <
block->top()) {
        player->setState(kPlayerDying);
        return;
      }
      break;
    }
  }
}
```

Similar steps are used to determine if we have a viable block or not.

If we do have a side collision, the `_player` state is changed to `kPlayerDying`, we reverse its x speed so the `_player` state will move to the left and off the screen, and we return from this method.

3. We end by updating the `_player` object's state based on our collision results:

```
if (inAir) {
    player->setState(kPlayerFalling);
} else {
    player->setState(kPlayerMoving);
    player->setFloating (false);
}
}
```

What just happened?

We just added the collision logic to our platform game. As we did in our first game, Air Hockey, we test the player's current position for collision as well as its next position to determine if a collision occurred between the current iteration and the next one. The test simply looks for overlaps between the player's and block's boundaries.

Adding the controls

It is fairly common in a dash game such as this to have very simple controls. Often the player must only press the screen for jumping. But we spiced things up a bit, adding a floating state.

And remember we want smooth transitions between states, so pay attention to how jumping is implemented: not by immediately applying a force to the player's vector but by simply changing a `boolean` property and letting the `_player` object's update method handle the change smoothly.

We'll handle the touch events next.

Time for action – handling touches

Let's go back to `GameLayer.cpp` and add our game's final touches (pun intended).

1. First we work on our `onTouchBegan` method:

    ```
    bool GameLayer::onTouchBegan(Touch* touch, Event* event) {

        if (!_running) {

            if (_player->getState() == kPlayerDying) {
                _terrain->reset();
                _player->reset();
                resetGame();
            }
            return true;
        }
    ```

    If we are not running the game and the _player object died, we reset the game on touch.

2. Next, if the terrain has not started, insert the following:

```
if (!_terrain->getStartTerrain()) {
  _terrain->setStartTerrain ( true );
  return true;
}
```

Remember that at first the buildings are all the same height and there are no gaps. Once the player presses the screen, we begin changing that through `setStartTerrain`.

3. We finish with:

```
if (touch) {
  if (_player->getState() == kPlayerFalling) {
      _player->setFloating ( _player->getFloating() ? false
: true );

  } else {

      if (_player->getState() != kPlayerDying) _player-
>setJumping(true);
  }
  return true;
}
return false;
}
```

Now we are in play, and if the `_player` object is falling, we either open or close the umbrella, whichever the case may be, through a call to `setFloating`.

And if the `_player` object is not falling, nor dying, we make it jump with `setJumping(true)`.

4. With touches ended, we just need to stop any jumps:

```
void GameLayer::onTouchEnded(Touch* touch, Event* event) {
    _player->setJumping(false);
}
```

What just happened?

We added the logic for the game's controls. The `_player` object will change to floating if currently falling or to jumping if currently riding on top of a building.

It's time to add our main game loop.

Time for action – coding the main loop

Finally, it's time for the last part in our logic.

1. Inside GameLayer.cpp:

    ```cpp
    void GameLayer::update(float dt) {

        if (!_running) return;


        if (_player->getPositionY() < -_player->getHeight() ||
            _player->getPositionX() < -_player->getWidth() * 0.5f)
            {

                _running = false;

        }
    ```

    If the _player object is off screen, we stop the game.

2. Now update all the elements, positions and check for collision:

    ```cpp
    _player->update(dt);

        _terrain->move(_player->getVector().x);

        if (_player->getState() != kPlayerDying)
            _terrain->checkCollision(_player);

        _player->place();
    ```

3. Move _gameBatchNode in relation to the _player object:

    ```cpp
    if (_player->getNextPosition().y > _screenSize.height * 0.6f) {
            _gameBatchNode->setPositionY( (_screenSize.height *
            0.6f - _player->getNextPosition().y) * 0.8f);

        } else {
            _gameBatchNode->setPositionY ( 0 );
        }
    ```

4. Make the game more difficult as time goes on by increasing the `_player` object's maximum speed:

```
if (_terrain->getStartTerrain() && _player->getVector().x > 0) {

        _speedIncreaseTimer += dt;
        if (_speedIncreaseTimer > _speedIncreaseInterval) {
            _speedIncreaseTimer = 0;
            _player->setMaxSpeed (_player->getMaxSpeed() + 4);
        }
    }


}
```

What just happened?

We have our test game in place. From here, we can test our terrain patterns, our speeds, and our general gameplay to find spots where things could be improved.

We should check in particular whether the game gets too hard too fast or whether we have combinations of buildings that are just impossible to get past.

I find, for instance, that starting with larger groups of buildings, say four or five, and then slowly reducing them to two and one between gaps can make the game even more fun to play, so the patterns could be changed to reflect that idea.

Summary

Every game has a simple idea for its gameplay at its core. But often, this idea needs a whole lot of testing and improvement before we can determine whether it's fun or not, which is why rapid prototyping is vital.

We can use Cocos2d-x to quickly test core gameplay ideas and run them in the simulator or on a device in a matter of minutes.

Also, the techniques shown here can be used to build interface elements (such as the energy bar from our previous game) as well as an entire game! If you don't believe me, check out the game *Square Ball* in an App Store near you.

Now, with all the logic for gameplay in its proper place, we can proceed to making this game look good! We'll do that in the next chapter.

7
Adding the Looks – Victorian Rush Hour

Now that we have our test game, it's time to make it all pretty! We'll go over the new sprite elements added to make the game look nice, and cover a new topic or two. However, by now, you should be able to understand everything in the final code of this project.

So you can sit back and relax a bit. This time, I won't make you type so much. Promise!

In this chapter, you will learn:

- How to use multiple sprites to texture a tiled terrain
- How to use multiple containers inside `SpriteBatchNode`
- How to create a parallax effect
- How to add a menu to your game
- How to build a game tutorial

Victorian Rush Hour – the game

Download the `4198_07_START_PROJECT.zip` file from this book's **Support** page (`www.packtpub.com/support`) and run the project in Xcode. You should be able to recognize all the work we did in the test version, and pinpoint the few extra elements. You will also see that nothing was added to the actual gameplay.

In *Victorian Rush Hour*, I wanted to make the terrain the main challenge in the game, but I also wanted to show you how easily you can add new elements to the buildings and interact with them.

You can later use the same logic to add enemies, obstacles, or pickups for the cyclist sprite. All you need to do really is extend the collision detection logic to check for the new items. You could, for instance, add umbrellas as pickups, and every time the `_player` object floated, he would be minus one umbrella.

Next, I'll list the new elements added to the game.

New sprites

Quite a few sprites were added to our game:

- There is a group of cyclists at the beginning of the game representing the traffic.
- We add a background layer (`cityscape`) and a foreground layer (`lamp posts`) to help us with our parallax effect. The clouds in the background are also part of the effect.
- We add chimneys to the buildings. These puff smoke as the player taps the screen.

◆ And, of course, the usual stuff—score label, game logo, and a game over message.

In the following screenshot, you can see an image of the player sprite and the group of cyclists:

Animations

Some of the sprites now run animation actions:

◆ The _player sprite runs an animation showing him riding the bicycle (_rideAnimation).

◆ I also added our old friend, the swinging animation, shown when the _player sprite is floating (_floatAnimation). This is the reason for the odd registration point on the cyclist sprite, as the swing animation looks better if the sprite's anchor point is not centered.

◆ Our group of cyclists is also animated during the introduction section of the game, and is moved offscreen when the game starts (_jamAnimate, _jamMove).

◆ We show a puff of smoke coming out of the chimneys whenever the player jumps. This animation is stored inside the new Block.cpp class and it's created through a series of actions, including a frame animation (_puffAnimation, _puffSpawn, _puffMove, _puffFade, and _puffScale).

◆ In GameLayer.cpp, when the _player object dies, we run a few actions on a _hat sprite to make it rise in the air and drop down again, just to add some humor.

Now let's go over the added logic.

Texturing our buildings with sprites

So in the test version we just coded, our game screen was divided into tiles of 128 pixels in the iPad retina screen. The width and height properties of the Block objects are based on this measurement. So a building two tiles wide and three tiles tall would have, in effect, 256 pixels in width and 384 pixels in height. A gap too would be measured this way, though its height is set to 0.

The logic we use to texture the buildings will take these tiles into account.

So let's take a look at the code to add texture to our buildings.

Time for action – texturing the buildings

There are a few changes to the way the `initBlock` method runs now:

1. Each block will store references to four different types of texture, representing the four types of buildings used in the game (`_tile1`, `_tile2`, `_tile3`, and `_tile4`). So we now store that information in the `initBlock` method:

    ```
    void Block::initBlock() {

      _tile1 = SpriteFrameCache::getInstance()-
    >getSpriteFrameByName ("building_1.png");
      _tile2 = SpriteFrameCache::getInstance()-
    >getSpriteFrameByName ("building_2.png");
      _tile3 = SpriteFrameCache::getInstance()-
    >getSpriteFrameByName ("building_3.png");
      _tile4 = SpriteFrameCache::getInstance()-
    >getSpriteFrameByName ("building_4.png");
    ```

2. Each block also stores references to two types of textures for the building roof tile (`_roof1` and `_roof2`):

    ```
    _roof1 = SpriteFrameCache::getInstance()->
    getSpriteFrameByName ("roof_1.png");
      _roof2 = SpriteFrameCache::getInstance()-
    >getSpriteFrameByName ("roof_2.png");
    ```

3. Next, we create and distribute the various sprite tiles that form our building:

    ```
    //create tiles
    for (int i = 0; i < 5; i++) {
        auto tile = Sprite::createWithSpriteFrameName("roof_1.png");
    ```

```
        tile->setAnchorPoint(Vec2(0, 1));
        tile->setPosition(Vec2(i * _tileWidth, 0));
        tile->setVisible(false);
        this->addChild(tile, kMiddleground, kRoofTile);
        _roofTiles.pushBack(tile);
        for (int j = 0; j < 4; j++) {
            tile =
Sprite::createWithSpriteFrameName("building_1.png");
            tile->setAnchorPoint(Vec2(0, 1));
            tile->setPosition(Vec2(i * _tileWidth, -1 *
(_tileHeight * 0.47f + j * _tileHeight)));
            tile->setVisible(false);
            this->addChild(tile, kBackground, kWallTile);
            _wallTiles.pushBack(tile);
        }
    }
}
```

A block comprises 20 sprites stored inside a _wallTiles vector and five sprites stored in a _roofTiles vector. So, when we initialize a Block object, we in effect create a building that is five tiles wide and four tiles tall. I made the decision that no building in the game would exceed this size. If you decide to change this, then here is where you would need to do it.

4. The initBlock method also creates five chimney sprites and places them at the top of the building. These will be spread out later according to the building type and could be very easily turned into obstacles for our _player sprite. We also create the animation actions for the puffs of smoke, here inside initBlock.

5. Moving on to our new setupBlock method, this is where the unnecessary tiles and chimneys are turned invisible and where we spread out the visible chimneys. We begin the method as follows:

```
void Block::setupBlock (int width, int height, int type) {

    this->setPuffing(false);

    _type = type;

    _width = width * _tileWidth;
    //add the roof height to the final height of the block
    _height = height * _tileHeight + _tileHeight * 0.49f;
    this->setPositionY(_height);
```

```
SpriteFrame * wallFrame;
SpriteFrame * roofFrame = rand() % 10 > 6 ? _roof1 :
_roof2;

int num_chimneys;
float chimneyX[] = {0,0,0,0,0};
```

6. Then, based on building type, we give different x positions for the chimney sprites and determine the texture we'll use on the wall tiles:

```
switch (type) {

    case kBlockGap:
        this->setVisible(false);
        return;

    case kBlock1:
        wallFrame = _tile1;
        chimneyX[0] = 0.2f;
        chimneyX[1] = 0.8f;
        num_chimneys = 2;
        break;
    case kBlock2:
        wallFrame = _tile2;
        chimneyX[0] = 0.2f;
         chimneyX[1] = 0.8f;
        chimneyX[2] = 0.5f;
        num_chimneys = 3;
        break;
    case kBlock3:
        wallFrame = _tile3;
        chimneyX[0] = 0.2f;
        chimneyX[1] = 0.8f;
        chimneyX[2] = 0.5f;
        num_chimneys = 3;

        break;
    case kBlock4:
        wallFrame = _tile4;
        chimneyX[0] = 0.2f;
        chimneyX[1] = 0.5f;
        num_chimneys = 2;
        break;
}
```

7. The method then proceeds to position the visible chimneys. And we finally move to texturing the building. The logic to texture the roof and wall tiles is the same; for instance, here's how the walls are tiled by changing the texture of each wall sprite through the `setDisplayFrame` method and then turning unused tiles invisible:

```
count = _wallTiles->count();
  for (i  = 0; i < count; i++) {
    tile = (Sprite *) _wallTiles->objectAtIndex(i);
    if (tile->getPositionX() < _width && tile
    ->getPositionY() > -_height) {
      tile->setVisible(true);
      tile->setDisplayFrame(wallFrame);
    } else {
      tile->setVisible(false);
    }
  }
}
```

What just happened?

When we instantiate a block in `initBlock`, we create a 5 x 4 building made out of wall tiles and roof tiles, each a sprite. And when we need to turn this building into a 3 x 2 building, or a 4 x 4 building, or whatever, we simply turn the excess tiles invisible at the end of `setupBlock`.

The texture used for the roof is picked randomly, but the one picked for the walls is based on building type (from our `patterns` array). It is also inside this `for` loop that all the tiles positioned at a point greater than the new building's width and height are turned invisible.

Containers within containers

Before we move to the parallax effect logic, there is something I wanted to talk about related to the layering of our `_gameBatchNode` object, which you'll recall is a `SpriteBatchNode` object.

If you go to the static `create` method inside `Terrain.cpp`, you will notice that the object is still created with a reference to a `blank.png` texture:

```
terrain->initWithSpriteFrameName("blank.png")
```

In fact, the same 1 x 1 pixel image used in the test version is now in our sprite sheet, only this time the image is transparent.

This is a bit of a hack, but necessary, because a sprite can only be placed inside a batch node if its texture source is the same used to create the batch node. But `Terrain` is just a container, it has no texture. However, by setting its `blank` texture to something contained in our sprite sheet, we can place `_terrain` inside `_gameBatchNode`.

The same thing is done with the `Block` class, which now, in the final version of the game, behaves like another textureless container. It will contain the various sprites for the wall and roof tiles as well as chimneys and puff animations as its children.

The organization of the layers inside our `_gameBatchNode` object can seem complex and at times even absurd. After all, in the same node, we have a foreground "layer" of lampposts, a middle-ground "layer" of buildings, and a background "layer" containing a cityscape. The player is also placed in the background but on top of the cityscape. Not only that, but all three layers are moved at different speeds to create our parallax effect, and all this inside the same `SpriteBatchNode`!

But the amount of code this arrangement saves us justifies any confusion we might have at times when attempting to keep the batch node organized. Now we can animate the puffs of smoke, for instance, and never worry about keeping them "attached" to their respective `chimney` sprite as the terrain scrolls to the left. The container will take care of keeping things together.

Creating a parallax effect

Cocos2d-x has a special node called `ParallaxNode`, and one surprising thing about it is how little you get to use it! `ParallaxNode` helps create a parallax effect with finite layers, or finite scrolling, which means that you can use it if your game screen has a limit to how much it can scroll each way. Implementing `ParallaxNode` to a game screen that can scroll indefinitely, such as the one in *Victorian Rush Hour*, usually requires more effort than it takes to build your own effect.

A parallax effect is created by moving objects at different depths at different speeds. The farther a layer appears from the screen, the slower its speed should be. In a game, this usually means that the player sprite's speed is fractioned to all the layers that appear behind it, and multiplied for the layers that appear in front of the player sprite:

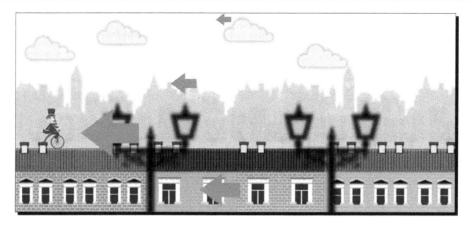

Let's add this to our game.

Time for action – creating a parallax effect

The parallax effect in our game takes place inside the main loop:

1. So in our `update` method, you will find the following lines of code:

```
if (_player->getVector().x > 0) {
  _background->setPositionX(_background->getPosition().x -
  _player->getVector().x * 0.25f);
```

First, we move the `_background` sprite, which contains the cityscape texture repeated three times along the x axis, and we move it at one-fourth of the speed of the `_player` sprite.

2. The `_background` sprite scrolls to the left, and as soon as the first cityscape texture is off the screen, we shift the entire `_background` container to the right at precisely the spot where the second cityscape texture would appear if allowed to continue. We get this value by subtracting where the sprite would be from the total width of the sprite:

```
float diffx;

if (_background->getPositionX() < -_background
  ->getContentSize().width) {
  diffx = fabs(_background->getPositionX()) - _background
  ->getContentSize().width;
  _background->setPositionX(-diffx);
}
```

So, in effect, we only ever scroll the first texture sprite inside the container.

3. A similar process is repeated with the `_foreground` sprite and the three lamppost sprites it contains. Only the `_foreground` sprite moves at four times the speed of the `_player` sprite. These are coded as follows:

```
_foreground->setPositionX(_foreground->getPosition().x - _player-
>getVector().x * 4);

if (_foreground->getPositionX() < -_foreground
  ->getContentSize().width * 4) {
  diffx = fabs(_foreground->getPositionX()) - _foreground
  ->getContentSize().width * 4;
  _foreground->setPositionX(-diffx);
}
```

4. We also employ our `cloud` sprites in the parallax effect. Since they appear behind the cityscape, so even farther away from `_player`, the clouds move at an even lower rate (`0.15`):

```
for (auto cloud : _clouds) {
    cloud->setPositionX(cloud->getPositionX() - _player-
>getVector().x * 0.15f);
    if (cloud->getPositionX() + cloud->getBoundingBox().size.width
* 0.5f < 0 ) {
        cloud->setPositionX(_screenSize.width + cloud-
>getBoundingBox().size.width * 0.5f);
    }
}
```

What just happened?

We just added the parallax effect in our game by simply using the player speed at different ratios at different depths. The only slightly complicated part of the logic is how to ensure the sprites scroll continuously. But the math of it is very simple. You just need to make sure the sprites align correctly.

Adding a menu to our game

Right now, we only see the game logo on our introduction screen. We need to add buttons to start the game and also for the option to play a tutorial.

In order to do that, we'll use a special kind of Layer class, called Menu.

Menu is a collection of MenuItems. The layer is responsible for distributing its items as well as tracking touch events on all items. Items can be sprites, labels, images, and so on.

Time for action – creating Menu and MenuItem

In GameLayer.cpp, scroll down to the createGameScreen method. We'll add the new logic to the end of this method.

1. First, create the menu item for our start game button:

```
auto menuItemOn =
Sprite::createWithSpriteFrameName("btn_new_on.png");
auto menuItemOff =
Sprite::createWithSpriteFrameName("btn_new_off.png");

auto starGametItem = MenuItemSprite::create( menuItemOff,
menuItemOn, CC_CALLBACK_1(GameLayer::startGame, this));
```

We create a MenuItemSprite object by passing it one sprite per state of the button. When the user touches a MenuItemSprite object, the off state sprite is turned invisible and the on state sprite is turned visible, all inside the touch began event. If the touch is ended or cancelled, the off state is displayed once again.

We also pass the callback function for this item; in this case, GameLayer::StartGame.

2. Next, we add the tutorial button:

```
menuItemOn =
Sprite::createWithSpriteFrameName("btn_howto_on.png");
menuItemOff =
Sprite::createWithSpriteFrameName("btn_howto_off.png");

auto howToItem = MenuItemSprite::create( menuItemOff,
menuItemOn, CC_CALLBACK_1(GameLayer::showTutorial, this));
```

3. Then it's time to create the menu:

```
_mainMenu = Menu::create(howToItem, starGametItem, nullptr);
_mainMenu->alignItemsHorizontallyWithPadding(120);
_mainMenu->setPosition(Vec2(_screenSize.width *
0.5f, _screenSize.height * 0.54));

this->addChild(_mainMenu, kForeground);
```

The `Menu` constructor can receive as many `MenuItemSprite` objects as you wish to display. These items are then distributed with one of the following calls: `alignItemsHorizontally`, `alignItemsHorizontallyWithPadding`, `alignItemsHorizontally`, `alignItemsVerticallyWithPadding`, `alignItemsInColumns`, and `alignItemsInRows`. And the items appear in the order they are passed to the `Menu` constructor.

4. Then we need to add our callback functions:

```
void GameLayer::startGame (Ref* pSender) {
  _tutorialLabel->setVisible(false);
  _intro->setVisible(false);
  _mainMenu->setVisible(false);

  _jam->runAction(_jamMove);
  SimpleAudioEngine::getInstance()
  ->playEffect("start.wav");
  _terrain->setStartTerrain ( true );
  _state = kGamePlay;
}

void GameLayer::showTutorial (Ref* pSender) {
  _tutorialLabel->setString
  ("Tap the screen to make the player jump.");
  _state = kGameTutorialJump;
  _jam->runAction(_jamMove);
  _intro->setVisible(false);
  _mainMenu->setVisible(false);
  SimpleAudioEngine::getInstance()
  ->playEffect("start.wav");
```

```
    _tutorialLabel->setVisible(true);

}
```

These are called when our menu buttons are clicked on, one method to start the game and one to show the tutorial.

What just happened?

We just created our game's main menu. Menu can save us a lot of time handling all the interactivity logic of buttons. Though it might not be as flexible as other items in Cocos2d-x, it's still good to know it's there if we need it.

We'll tackle the tutorial section next.

Adding a tutorial to our game

Let's face it. With the possible exception of *Air Hockey*, every game so far in this book could benefit from a tutorial, or a "how to play" section. With *Victorian Rush Hour*, I'm going to show you a quick way to implement one.

The unspoken rule of game tutorials is—make it playable. And that's what we'll attempt to do here.

We'll create a game state for our tutorial, and we'll add a Label object to our stage and make it invisible unless the tutorial state is on. We'll use the Label object to display our tutorial text, as shown in the image here:

Let's go over the steps necessary to create our game tutorial.

Time for action – adding a tutorial

Let's move back to our `createGameScreen` method.

1. Inside that method, add the following lines to create our `Label` object:

```
_tutorialLabel = Label::createWithTTF("", "fonts/Times.ttf", 60);
_tutorialLabel->setPosition(Vec2 (_screenSize.width *
0.5f, _screenSize.height * 0.6f) );
this->addChild(_tutorialLabel, kForeground);
_tutorialLabel->setVisible(false);
```

2. We add four states to our enumerated list of game states. These will represent the different steps in our tutorial:

```
typedef enum {
    kGameIntro,
    kGamePlay,
    kGameOver,
    kGameTutorial,
    kGameTutorialJump,
    kGameTutorialFloat,
    kGameTutorialDrop

} GameState;
```

The first tutorial state, `kGameTutorial`, acts as a separator from all other game states. So, if the value for `_state` is greater than `kGameTutorial`, we are in tutorial mode.

Now, depending on the mode, we display a different message and we wait on a different condition to change to a new tutorial state.

3. If you recall, our `showTutorial` method starts with a message telling the player to tap the screen to make the sprite jump:

```
_tutorialLabel->setString
    ("Tap the screen to make the player jump.");
_state = kGameTutorialJump;
```

4. Then, at the end of the `update` method, we start adding the lines that will display the rest of our tutorial information. First, if the player sprite is in the midst of a jump and has just begun falling, we use the following:

```
if (_state > kGameTutorial) {
    if (_state == kGameTutorialJump) {
```

```
if (_player->getState() == kPlayerFalling && _player
->getVector().y < 0) {
  _player->stopAllActions();
  _jam->setVisible(false);
  _jam->stopAllActions();
  _running = false;
  _tutorialLabel->setString
  ("While in the air, tap the screen to float.");
  _state = kGameTutorialFloat;
}
```

As you can see, we let the player know that another tap will open the umbrella and cause the sprite to float.

5. Next, as the sprite is floating, when it reaches a certain distance from the buildings, we inform the player that another tap will close the umbrella and cause the sprite to drop. Here's the code for these instructions:

```
} else if (_state == kGameTutorialFloat) {
  if (_player->getPositionY() < _screenSize.height *
  0.95f) {
    _player->stopAllActions();
    _running = false;
    _tutorialLabel->setString
    ("While floating, tap the screen again to drop.");
    _state = kGameTutorialDrop;
  }
```

6. After that, the tutorial will be complete and we show the message that the player may start the game:

```
} else {
  _tutorialLabel->setString
  ("That's it. Tap the screen to play.");
  _state = kGameTutorial;
}
}
```

Whenever we change a tutorial state, we pause the game momentarily and wait for a tap. We handle the rest of our logic inside onTouchBegan, so we'll add that next.

7. Inside onTouchBegan, in the switch statement, add the following cases:

```
case kGameTutorial:
  _tutorialLabel->setString("");
  _tutorialLabel->setVisible(false);
```

```
   _terrain->setStartTerrain ( true );
   _state = kGamePlay;
   break;

case kGameTutorialJump:
   if (_player->getState() == kPlayerMoving) {
     SimpleAudioEngine::getInstance()
     ->playEffect("jump.wav");
     _player->setJumping(true);
   }
   break;

case kGameTutorialFloat:
   if (!_player->getFloating()) {
     _player->setFloating (true);
     _running = true;
   }
   break;

case kGameTutorialDrop:
   _player->setFloating (false);
   _running = true;
   break;
```

What just happened?

We added a tutorial to our game! As you can see, we used quite a few new states. But now we can incorporate the tutorial right into our game and have one flow smoothly into the other. All these changes can be seen in action in the final version of this project, `4198_07_FINAL_PROJECT.zip`, which you can find on this book's **Support** page.

Now, you guessed it, let's run it in Android.

Time for action – running the game in Android

Follow these steps to deploy the game to Android:

1. Open your project's `Android.mk` file in a text editor.

2. Edit the lines in `LOCAL_SRC_FILES` to read:

```
LOCAL_SRC_FILES := hellocpp/main.cpp \
                   ../../Classes/AppDelegate.cpp \
                   ../../Classes/Block.cpp \
```

```
../../Classes/GameSprite.cpp \
../../Classes/Player.cpp \
../../Classes/Terrain.cpp \
../../Classes/GameLayer.cpp
```

3. Import the game into Eclipse and wait until all classes are compiled.

4. That's it. Save it and run your application.

What just happened?

You now have *Victorian Rush Hour* running in Android.

Summary

After we got all the gameplay details ironed out in our test game, bringing in a sprite sheet and game states seems remarkably simple and easy.

But during this stage, we can also think of new ways to improve gameplay. For instance, the realization that clouds of smoke coming out of chimneys would offer a nice visual cue to the player to identify where the buildings were, if the cyclist happened to jump too high. Or that a hat flying through the air could be funny!

Now it's time to bring physics to our games, so head on to the next chapter.

8

Getting Physical – Box2D

It's time to tackle physics! Cocos2d-x comes bundled with Box2D and Chipmunk. These are so-called 2D physics engines – the first written in C++ and the second in C. Chipmunk has a more recent Objective-C port but Cocos2d-x must use the original one written in C for portability.

We'll be using Box2D for the examples in this book. The next two games I'll show you will be developed with that engine, starting with a simple pool game to illustrate all the main points about using Box2D in your projects.

In this chapter, you will learn:

- How to set up and run a Box2D simulation
- How to create bodies
- How to use the debug draw feature to quickly test your concepts
- How to use collision filters and listeners

Building a Box2D project with Cocos2d-x

With version 3.x of the framework, we no longer need to specify that we want to use a physics engine. The projects add these APIs by default. So, all you need in order to create a Box2D project is to create a regular Cocos2d-x project as we've been doing with the examples so far.

There is, however, one extra step you need to perform if you wish to use something called a debug draw in your project. So let's set that up now.

Time for action – using debug draw in your Box2D project

Let's start by creating the project. In my machine, I created a game called MiniPool in my desktop. Here are the steps:

1. Open Terminal and enter the following command:

   ```
   cocos new MiniPool -p com.rengelbert.MiniPool -l cpp -d /Users/
   rengelbert/Desktop/MiniPool
   ```

2. Open the new project in Xcode.

3. Now navigate to the `Tests` folder inside the Cocos2d-x framework folder. This can be found in `tests/cpp-tests/Classes`. Then open the `Box2DTestBed` folder.

4. Drag the files `GLES-Render.h` and `GLES-Render.cpp` to your project in Xcode.

5. You can also open the `Box2dTest.cpp` class in the test folder `Box2DTest`, as we're going to copy and paste a few of the methods from there.

6. In the `HelloWorldScene.h` header file, leave the includes in place, but change the class declarations to match these:

   ```cpp
   class HelloWorld : public cocos2d::Layer {
   public:
       virtual ~HelloWorld();
       HelloWorld();

       static cocos2d::Scene* scene();

       void initPhysics();
       void update(float dt);
       virtual void draw(Renderer *renderer, const Mat4 &transform,
   uint32_t flags) override;

   private:
       GLESDebugDraw * _debugDraw;
       b2World* world;
       Mat4 _modelViewMV;
       void onDraw();
       CustomCommand _customCommand;
   };
   ```

7. Then add this `include` statement at the top:

   ```cpp
   #include "GLES-Render.h"
   ```

8. Then, in the `HelloWorldScene.cpp` implementation file, replace the lines between the `using namespace CocosDenshion` and `HelloWorld::scene` methods with these:

```
#define PTM_RATIO 32

HelloWorld::HelloWorld()
{
    this->initPhysics();
    scheduleUpdate();
}

HelloWorld::~HelloWorld()
{
    delete world;
    world = nullptr;

    delete _debugDraw;
    _debugDraw = nullptr;
}

void HelloWorld::initPhysics() {

    b2Vec2 gravity;
    gravity.Set(0.0f, -10.0f);
    world = new b2World(gravity);

    // Do we want to let bodies sleep?
    world->SetAllowSleeping(true);
    world->SetContinuousPhysics(true);

    _debugDraw = new (std::nothrow) GLESDebugDraw( PTM_RATIO );
    world->SetDebugDraw(_debugDraw);

    uint32 flags = 0;
    flags += b2Draw::e_shapeBit;
    //       flags += b2Draw::e_jointBit;
    //       flags += b2Draw::e_aabbBit;
    //       flags += b2Draw::e_pairBit;
    //       flags += b2Draw::e_centerOfMassBit;
    _debugDraw->SetFlags(flags);

}
```

```
void HelloWorld::update(float dt)
{
    world->Step(dt, 8, 1);


}
```

9. Now comes the implementation of the `draw` methods. You can copy and paste most of this code from the `Box2DTest` folder:

```
void GameLayer::draw(Renderer *renderer, const Mat4 &transform,
uint32_t flags)
{
    //
    // IMPORTANT:
    // This is only for debug purposes
    // It is recommended to disable it
    //
    Layer::draw(renderer, transform, flags);
    GL::enableVertexAttribs( cocos2d::GL::VERTEX_ATTRIB_FLAG_
POSITION );
    auto director = Director::getInstance();
    CCASSERT(nullptr != director, "Director is null when setting
matrix stack");
    director->pushMatrix(MATRIX_STACK_TYPE::MATRIX_STACK_
MODELVIEW);

    _modelViewMV = director->getMatrix(MATRIX_STACK_TYPE::MATRIX_
STACK_MODELVIEW);

    _customCommand.init(_globalZOrder);
    _customCommand.func = CC_CALLBACK_0(GameLayer::onDraw, this);
    renderer->addCommand(&_customCommand);

    director->popMatrix(MATRIX_STACK_TYPE::MATRIX_STACK_
MODELVIEW);

}

void GameLayer::onDraw()
{
    auto director = Director::getInstance();
    Mat4 oldMV;
    oldMV = director->getMatrix(MATRIX_STACK_TYPE::MATRIX_STACK_
MODELVIEW);
```

```
        director->loadMatrix(MATRIX_STACK_TYPE::MATRIX_STACK_
MODELVIEW, _modelViewMV);
        _world->DrawDebugData();
        director->loadMatrix(MATRIX_STACK_TYPE::MATRIX_STACK_
MODELVIEW, oldMV);
    }
```

What just happened?

The GLES-Render class is necessary to use the debug draw feature in Box2D. This will draw all the elements from the simulation on the screen. The debug draw object is created inside the initPhysics method alongside the Box2D simulation (b2World). We'll go over that logic in a moment.

As the comment inside the draw method states, the debug draw feature should be switched off once you're done developing your game. So all the lines pertaining to that object as well as the draw method should be commented out when you're ready for a release version.

So what is a physics engine?

The famous Isaac Newton said, *every action has a reaction*. Right after he said, *who the hell threw that apple?*

So far in our games, we have covered very simple collision systems, basically only ever checking to see if simple shapes (circles and rectangles) overlapped each other. The reactions from these collisions were also very simple in our games so far: with vector inversions or simply by making things disappear once they touch. With Box2D, you get way more!

Box2D is a very robust collision detection engine and can certainly be used just for that purpose. But the simulation will also process and return a bunch of information derived from the collisions and the interactions between bodies, meaning how the objects should behave, based on their shapes, mass, and all the forces at play in the simulation.

Meeting Box2D

At the core of the engine, you have the b2World object. This is the simulation. You fill the world with b2Body objects, and then you step through the simulation with b2World->Step(). And you take the results of the simulation and display them to the user through your sprites, by grabbing a b2Body object's position and rotation and applying them to a sprite.

The debug draw object allows you to see the simulation without using any sprites. Sort of like a version of our test project from *Chapter 6*, *Quick and Easy Sprite – Victorian Rush Hour*.

Meeting the world

Most of the time, the physics simulation will mean the creation of a `b2World` object. Note, however, that you *can* get interesting results managing more than one `world` object in the same game, for multiple views for instance. But that's for another book.

In our simplified basic project, the world is created like this:

```
b2Vec2 gravity;
gravity.Set(0.0f, -10.0f);
world = new b2World(gravity);

// Do we want to let bodies sleep?
world->SetAllowSleeping(true);
world->SetContinuousPhysics(true);

_debugDraw = new (std::nothrow) GLESDebugDraw( PTM_RATIO );
world->SetDebugDraw(_debugDraw);

uint32 flags = 0;
flags += b2Draw::e_shapeBit;
//          flags += b2Draw::e_jointBit;
//          flags += b2Draw::e_aabbBit;
//          flags += b2Draw::e_pairBit;
//          flags += b2Draw::e_centerOfMassBit;
_debugDraw->SetFlags(flags);
```

Box2D has its own vector structure, `b2Vec2`, and we use it here to create the world's gravity. The `b2World` object receives that as its parameter. A simulation does not always require gravity, of course; in that case, the argument will be a `(0, 0)` vector.

`SetAllowSleeping` means if objects are not moving and therefore not generating derived data, skip checking for derived data from those objects.

`SetContinuousPhysics` means we have some fast objects in our hands, which we'll later point out to the simulation, so it can pay extra attention for collisions.

Then we create the debug draw object. This is optional, as I said before. The flags indicate what you wish to see in the drawing. In the code we saw before, we only want to see the shapes of the objects.

Then comes `PTM_RATIO`, the defined constant we passed as a parameter to the debug draw. Box2D uses meters instead of pixels for a variety of reasons that are really entirely unnecessary for anyone to know. Except for one reason, **pixel to meter (PTM)**, so every pixel position value used in the game will be divided by this ratio constant. If the result from this division ever gets above 10 or below 0.1, increase or decrease the value for `PTM_RATIO` accordingly.

You have some leeway, of course. By all means, play with this value once your game is completed, and pay special attention to the subtle differences in speed (another common value for this ratio is 100).

Running the simulation

As I said before, you use the `Step` method to run the simulation, usually inside your main loop, though not necessarily:

```
world->Step(dt, 8, 1);
```

You need to pass it the time step, here represented by the delta time in the main loop. Then pass the number of velocity iterations and position iterations in the step. This basically means how many times velocity and position will be processed inside a step.

In the previous example, I'm using the default values from the Box2D template in Cocos2d-x. Usually, a fixed time step is better than the delta, and a higher value for position iteration may be necessary if things move really fast in your game. But always remember to play with these values, aiming at finding the lowest possible ones.

No Ref objects in Box2D

Box2D does not use `Ref` objects. So, no memory management! Remember to get rid of all the Box2D objects through `delete` and not `release`. If you knew it already... well, you remember:

```
HelloWorld::~HelloWorld(){
    delete world;
    world = nullptr;

    delete _debugDraw;
    _debugDraw = nullptr;
}
```

As I mentioned before, C++11 introduces smart pointers, which are memory managed, meaning you *don't* have to delete these objects yourself. However, the topic of shared pointers is beyond the scope of this book, and using unique pointers in this chapter would add way too many lines that had nothing to do with Box2D. And although smart pointers are amazing, their syntax and usage is, well, let's say very "C++ish".

Meeting the bodies

The b2Body object is the thing you'll spend most of your time dealing with inside a Box2D simulation. You have three main types of b2Bodies: dynamic, static, and kinematic. The first two are of greater importance and are the ones we'll use in our game.

Bodies are created by combining a body definition with a body fixture. The body definition is a structure that holds information about type, position, velocity, and angle, among other things. The fixture holds information about the shape, including its density, elasticity, and friction.

So, to create a circle that is 40 pixels wide, you would use the following:

```
b2BodyDef bodyDef;
bodyDef.type = b2_dynamicBody;
//or make it static bodyDef.type = b2_staticBody;
b2Body * body = world->CreateBody(&bodyDef);

//create circle shape
b2CircleShape  circle;
circle.m_radius = 20.0/PTM_RATIO;

//define fixture
b2FixtureDef fixtureDef;
fixtureDef.shape = &circle;
fixtureDef.density = 1;
fixtureDef.restitution = 0.7;
fixtureDef.friction = 0.4;

body->CreateFixture(&fixtureDef);
```

To create a box that is 40 pixels wide, you would use this:

```
//create body
b2BodyDef bodyDef;
bodyDef.type = b2_dynamicBody;
b2Body * body = world->CreateBody(&bodyDef);

//define shape
b2PolygonShape box;
box.SetAsBox(20 /PTM_RATIO, 20 / PTM_RATIO);

//Define fixture
b2FixtureDef fixtureDef;
```

```
fixtureDef.shape = &box;
fixtureDef.density = 2;
fixtureDef.restitution = 0;
body->CreateFixture(&fixtureDef);
```

Note that you use the `world` object to create the bodies. And also note that boxes are created with half their desired width and height.

Density, friction, and restitution all have default values, so you don't always need to set these.

Our game – MiniPool

Our game consists of sixteen balls (circles), one cue (box), and a pool table made out of six lines (edges) and six pockets (circles). This is all there is to it as far as the Box2D simulation is concerned.

Download the final project from this book's **Support** page if you wish to follow along with the final code. Box2D is a complex API and it will be best to review and expose the logic rather than work on it by doing a lot of typing. So there will be no start project to work from this time. You may choose any manner to add files from the finished project to the one we started when I showed you how to set up the debug draw object. The final game will look like this:

Game settings

This is a portrait-orientation-only game, with no screen rotation allowed, and universal application. The game is designed for the regular iPhone (320 x 480) and its resolution size is set to kResolutionShowAll. This will show borders around the main screen in devices that do not match the 1.5 screen ratio of the iPhone.

```cpp
//in AppDelegate.cpp
auto screenSize = glview->getFrameSize();
auto designSize = Size(320, 480);

glview->setDesignResolutionSize(designSize.width, designSize.height,
ResolutionPolicy::SHOW_ALL);
std::vector<std::string> searchPaths;
    if (screenSize.width > 640) {
        searchPaths.push_back("ipadhd");
        director->setContentScaleFactor(1280/designSize.width);
    } else if (screenSize.width > 320) {
        searchPaths.push_back("ipad");
        director->setContentScaleFactor(640/designSize.width);
    } else {
        searchPaths.push_back("iphone");
        director->setContentScaleFactor(320/designSize.width);
    }
    auto fileUtils = FileUtils::getInstance();
    fileUtils->setSearchPaths(searchPaths);
```

Note that I use the iPhone's dimensions to identify larger screens. So the iPad and the iPhone retina are considered to be two times 320 x 480 and the retina iPad is considered to be four times 320 x 480.

Sprite plus b2Body equal to b2Sprite

The most common way to work with b2Body objects in Cocos2d-x is to combine them with sprites. In the games I'll show you, I created a class called b2Sprite that extends sprite with the addition of a _body member property that points to its very own b2Body. I also add a few helper methods to deal with our pesky PTM_RATIO. Feel free to add as many of these as you think necessary.

b2Body objects have an incredibly helpful property called userData. You can store anything you wish inside it and the bodies will carry it with them throughout the simulation. So, what most developers do is that they store inside the body's userData property a reference to the instance of sprite wrapping it. So b2Sprite knows about its body, and the body knows about its b2Sprite.

As a matter of fact, composition is key when working with Box2D. So, when designing your games, make sure every object knows of every other object or can get to them quickly. This will help immensely.

Creating the pool table

In the debug draw view, this is what the table looks like:

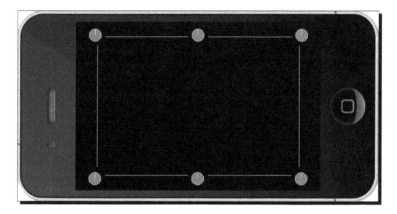

All the elements seen here are created inside the initPhysics method in GameLayer.cpp. The table has no visual representation other than the background image we use in the game. So there are no sprites attached to the individual pockets, for example.

The pocket bodies are created inside a for loop, with the best algorithm I could come up with to distribute them correctly on screen. This logic is found in the initPhysics method, so let's take a look at that and see how our first b2Body objects are created:

```
b2Body * pocket;
b2CircleShape circle;
float startX = _screenSize.width * 0.07;
float startY = _screenSize.height * 0.92f;
for (int i = 0; i < 6; i++) {
    bodyDef.type = b2_staticBody;
    if (i < 3) {
        bodyDef.position.Set(startX/PTM_RATIO,
(startY - i * (_screenSize.height * 0.84f * 0.5f))/PTM_RATIO);

    } else {
```

```
        bodyDef.position.Set(
        (startX + _screenSize.width * 0.85f)/PTM_RATIO,
        (startY - (i-3) * (_screenSize.height * 0.84f *
        0.5f))/PTM_RATIO);
    }
    pocket = _world->CreateBody(&bodyDef);
    fixtureDef.isSensor = true;
    circle.m_radius = (float) (1.5 * BALL_RADIUS) / PTM_RATIO;
    fixtureDef.shape = &circle;

    pocket->CreateFixture(&fixtureDef);
    auto pocketData = new b2Sprite(this, kSpritePocket);
    pocket->SetUserData(pocketData);
}
```

The `pocket` bodies are static bodies and we determine in their fixture definition that they should behave like sensors:

```
fixtureDef.isSensor = true;
```

This switches off all the physics from an object and turns it into a collision hot spot. A sensor serves only to determine if something is touching it or not.

 It's almost always best to ignore Box2D sensors and use your own sprites or points in your collision logic. One neat feature in sensors is that they make it very easy to determine when something has just ceased touching them, as you'll see once we cover contact listeners.

Creating edges

If a shape can only be hit on one side, an edge is probably what you need. Here is how we create edges in our game:

```
b2BodyDef tableBodyDef;
tableBodyDef.position.Set(0, 0);
b2Body* tableBody = _world->CreateBody(&tableBodyDef);

// Define the table edges
b2EdgeShape tableBox;

// bottom edge
tableBox.Set(b2Vec2(_screenSize.width * 0.14f/PTM_RATIO, _screenSize.
height * 0.09f/PTM_RATIO),
```

```
b2Vec2(_screenSize.width * 0.86f/PTM_RATIO, _screenSize.height *
0.09f/PTM_RATIO));
tableBody->CreateFixture(&tableBox,0);

// top edge
tableBox.Set(b2Vec2(_screenSize.width * 0.14f/PTM_RATIO, _screenSize.
height * 0.91f/PTM_RATIO),
    b2Vec2(_screenSize.width * 0.86f/PTM_RATIO, _screenSize.height *
0.91f/PTM_RATIO));
tableBody->CreateFixture(&tableBox,0);
```

So the same `b2Body` object can have as many edges as you need. You set an edge with its start and end points (in this case, the `b2Vec2` structures) and add it as a fixture to the body, with a density of `0`.

Creating the ball objects

In the game, there is a class called `Ball` that extends `b2Sprite`, used for both the target balls and the cue ball. These objects are also created inside the `initPhysics` method. Here is the basic configuration of that object:

```
//create Box2D body
b2BodyDef bodyDef;
bodyDef.type = b2_dynamicBody;

_body = _game->getWorld()->CreateBody(&bodyDef);
_body->SetLinearDamping(1.2f);
_body->SetAngularDamping(0.2f);

//create circle shape
b2CircleShape  circle;
circle.m_radius = BALL_RADIUS/PTM_RATIO;

//define fixture
b2FixtureDef fixtureDef;
fixtureDef.shape = &circle;
fixtureDef.density = 5;
fixtureDef.restitution = 0.7f;

//add collision filters so only white ball can be hit by cue
if (_type == kSpriteBall) {
    fixtureDef.filter.categoryBits = 0x0010;
} else if (_type == kSpritePlayer) {
```

```
//white ball is tracked as bullet by simulation
    _body->SetBullet(true);
    fixtureDef.filter.categoryBits = 0x0100;
}

//set sprite texture
switch (_color) {
    case kColorBlack:
        this->initWithSpriteFrameName("ball_black.png");
        break;
    case kColorRed:
        this->initWithSpriteFrameName("ball_red.png");
        break;
    case kColorYellow:
        this->initWithSpriteFrameName("ball_yellow.png");
        break;
    case kColorWhite:
        this->initWithSpriteFrameName("ball_white.png");
        break;
}

_body->CreateFixture(&fixtureDef);
//store the b2Sprite as the body's userData
_body->SetUserData(this);
```

The `friction` fixture property involves the reaction of two touching surfaces (two bodies). In this case, we want to create "friction" with the table surface, which is not a body at all. So what we need to use instead is **damping**. This will apply a similar effect to friction, but without the need for an extra surface. Damping can be applied to the linear velocity vector of a body as follows:

```
_body->SetLinearDamping(1.2);
```

And to the angular velocity as follows:

```
_body->SetAngularDamping(0.2);
```

Also, the white ball is set to be a bullet:

```
_body->SetBullet(true);
```

This will make the simulation pay extra attention to this object in terms of collision. We could make all balls in the game behave as bullets, but this is not only unnecessary (something revealed through testing) but also not very processing-friendly.

Creating collision filters

In the `ball` object, there is a `filter` property inside the fixture definition that we use to mask collisions. Meaning we determine what bodies can collide with each other. The cue ball receives a different value for `categoryBits` than the other balls.

```
fixtureDef.filter.categoryBits = 0x0100;
```

When we create the cue body, we set a `maskBits` property in its fixture definition as follows:

```
fixtureDef.filter.maskBits = 0x0100;
```

We set this to the same value as the white ball's `categoryBits`.

The result of all this? Now the cue can only hit bodies with the same `categoryBits`, which here means the cue can only collide with the white ball.

It is possible to add more than one category to a mask with a bitwise | option, as seen here:

```
fixtureDef.filter.maskBits = 0x0100 | 0x0010;
```

Or to collide with everything except the cue ball, for instance, as seen in the following line:

```
fixtureDef.filter.maskBits = 0xFFFF & ~0x0100;
```

Creating the cue

The cue ball also extends `b2Sprite`, and its body is set as a box.

```
//create body
b2BodyDef bodyDef;
bodyDef.type = b2_dynamicBody;

_body = _game->getWorld()->CreateBody(&bodyDef);
_body->SetLinearDamping(8);
_body->SetAngularDamping(5);

//Define shape
b2PolygonShape box;
box.SetAsBox(BALL_RADIUS * 21 /PTM_RATIO, BALL_RADIUS * 0.2 / PTM_
RATIO);

//Define fixture
b2FixtureDef fixtureDef;
fixtureDef.shape = &box;
```

```
fixtureDef.filter.maskBits = 0x0100;
fixtureDef.density = 10;
fixtureDef.restitution = 1;
_body->CreateFixture(&fixtureDef);
_body->SetUserData(this);
```

It has very high damping values because, in the rare occasions when the player misses the cue ball, the cue will not fly off the screen but halt a few pixels from the white ball.

If we wanted to create the cue ball as a trapezium or a triangle, we would need to give the b2PolygonShape option the vertices we want. Here's an example of this:

```
b2Vec2 vertices[3];
vertices[0].Set(0.0f, 0.0f);
vertices[1].Set(1.0f, 0.0f);
vertices[2].Set(0.0f, 1.0f);
int32 count = 3;

b2PolygonShape triangle;
triangle.Set(vertices, count);
```

And the vertices must be added counterclockwise to the array. Meaning, if we add the top vertex of the triangle first, the next vertex must be the one to the left.

Once all the elements are in place, the debug draw looks like this:

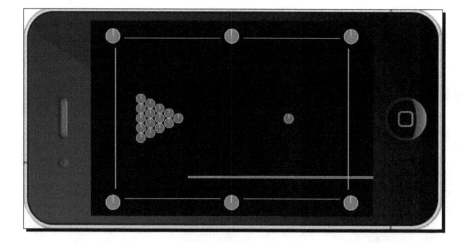

Creating a contact listener

Besides collision filters, one other feature in Box2D that helps with collision management is the creation of a contact listener.

Inside the `initPhysics` method, we create the `world` object like this:

```
b2Vec2 gravity;
gravity.Set(0.0f, 0.0f);
_world = new b2World(gravity);

_world->SetAllowSleeping(true);
_world->SetContinuousPhysics(true);
_collisionListener = new CollisionListener();
_world->SetContactListener(_collisionListener);
```

Our `CollisionListener` class extends the Box2D `b2ContactListener` class, and it must implement at least one of the following methods:

◆   `void BeginContact(b2Contact* contact);`

◆   `void EndContact(b2Contact* contact);`

◆   `void PreSolve(b2Contact* contact, const b2Manifold* oldManifold);`

◆   `void PostSolve(b2Contact* contact, const b2ContactImpulse* impulse);`

These events are all related to a contact (collision) and are fired at different stages of a contact.

 Sensor objects can only ever fire the `BeginContact` and `EndContact` events.

In our game, we implement two of these methods. The first is:

```
void CollisionListener::BeginContact(b2Contact* contact) {
    b2Body * bodyA = contact->GetFixtureA()->GetBody();
    b2Body * bodyB = contact->GetFixtureB()->GetBody();

    b2Sprite * spriteA = (b2Sprite *) bodyA->GetUserData();
    b2Sprite * spriteB = (b2Sprite *) bodyB->GetUserData();

    if (spriteA && spriteB) {
```

```
                //track collision between balls and pockets
                if (spriteA->getType() == kSpritePocket) {
                    spriteB->setVisible(false);
                } else if (spriteB->getType() == kSpritePocket) {
                    spriteA->setVisible(false);
                } else if (spriteA->getType() == kSpriteBall &&
                    spriteB->getType() == kSpriteBall) {
                    if (spriteA->mag() > 10 || spriteB->mag() > 10) {
                    SimpleAudioEngine::getInstance()-
                    >playEffect("ball.wav");
                    }
                } else if ((spriteA->getType() == kSpriteBall &&
                        spriteB->getType() == kSpritePlayer) ||
                        (spriteB->getType() == kSpriteBall &&
                        spriteA->getType() == kSpritePlayer)) {
                    if (spriteA->mag() > 10 || spriteB->mag() > 10) {
                        SimpleAudioEngine::getInstance()-
                        >playEffect("ball.wav");
                    }
                }
            }
        }
    }
```

You can see now how important the userData property is. We can quickly access sprites attached to the bodies listed in the b2Contact object through the userData property.

Besides that, all our sprites have a _type property that behaves like identifying tags in our logic. Note that you could certainly use the Cocos2d-x tags for that, but I find that at times, if you can combine the Sprite tags with their _type value, you may produce interesting sorting logic.

So, in BeginContact, we track the collisions between balls and pockets. But we also track collision between balls. In the first case, the balls are turned invisible when they touch the pockets. And, in the second case, we play a sound effect whenever two balls touch each other, but only if they are at a certain speed (we determine that through a b2Sprite helper method that retrieves the squared magnitude of a sprite's velocity vector).

The other method in our listener is:

```
    void CollisionListener::PreSolve(b2Contact* contact, const b2Manifold*
    oldManifold)  {

        b2Body * bodyA = contact->GetFixtureA()->GetBody();
        b2Body * bodyB = contact->GetFixtureB()->GetBody();
```

```
b2Sprite * spriteA = (b2Sprite *) bodyA->GetUserData();
b2Sprite * spriteB = (b2Sprite *) bodyB->GetUserData();


if (spriteA && spriteB) {

//track collision between player and cue ball
    if (spriteA->getType() == kSpriteCue && spriteA->mag() > 2) {
        if (spriteB->getType() == kSpritePlayer && spriteA-
        >isVisible()) {
            SimpleAudioEngine::getInstance()-
            >playEffect("hit.wav");
            spriteA->setVisible(false);
            spriteB->getGame()->setCanShoot(false);
        }
    } else if (spriteB->getType() == kSpriteCue && spriteA->mag()
    > 2) {
        if (spriteA->getType() == kSpritePlayer && spriteB-
        >isVisible()) {
            SimpleAudioEngine::getInstance()-
            >playEffect("hit.wav");
            spriteB->setVisible(false);
            spriteA->getGame()->setCanShoot(false);
        }
    }
}

}
}
```

Here, we listen to a collision before its reactions are calculated. If there is a collision between the cue and white ball, we play a sound effect and we hide the cue.

If you want to force your own logic to the collision reaction and override Box2D on this, you should do so in the `PreSolve` method. In this game, however, we could have added all this collision logic to the `BeginContact` method and it would work just as well.

The game controls

In the game, the player must click on the white ball and then drag his or her finger to activate the cue ball. The farther the finger gets from the white ball, the more powerful the shot will be.

So let's add the events to handle user input.

Time for action – adding the touch events

We'll deal with onTouchBegan first.

1. In the onTouchBegan method, we start by updating the game state:

```
bool GameLayer::onTouchBegan(Touch * touch, Event * event) {

    if (!_running) return true;

    if (_gameState == kGameOver) {
        if (_gameOver->isVisible()) _gameOver->setVisible(false);
        resetGame();
        return true;
    }
```

2. Next, we check on the value of _canShoot. This returns true if the white ball is not moving.

```
if (!_canShoot) return true;
```

3. Next, we determine whether the touch is landing on the white ball. If it is, we start the game if it is not currently running yet and we make our timer visible. Here's the code to do this:

```
if (touch) {

    auto tap = touch->getLocation();
    auto playerPos = _player->getPosition();
    float diffx = tap.x - playerPos.x;
    float diffy = tap.y - playerPos.y;
    float diff = pow(diffx, 2) + pow(diffy, 2);
    if (diff < pow(BALL_RADIUS * 4, 2)) {
        if (_gameState != kGamePlay) {
            _gameState = kGamePlay;
            if (_intro->isVisible()) _intro->setVisible(false);
            _timer->setVisible(true);
        }
    }
}
```

Note that we use a larger radius for the white ball in our logic (four times larger). This is because we don't want the target area to be too small, since this game will run on both iPhones and iPads. We want the player to comfortably hit the white ball with his or her finger.

4. We store where in the ball the point lies. This way, the player can hit the ball at different spots, causing it to move at different angles:

```
//make point lie within ball
if (diff > pow(BALL_RADIUS * 2, 2)) {
    float angle = atan2(diffy, diffx);
    _cueStartPoint = Vec2(
            playerPos.x + BALL_RADIUS * 0.8f * cos(angle),
            playerPos.y + BALL_RADIUS * 0.8f * sin(angle));
} else {
    _cueStartPoint = playerPos;
}
```

Since we made the white ball a much larger target for our `touch` event, now we must make sure the actual point picked by the player lies within the ball. So we may have to make some adjustments here.

5. We pass the point to our `LineContainer` object and we prepare the cue body to be used, as follows:

```
_lineContainer->setBallPoint(_cueStartPoint);
_cue->getBody()->SetLinearVelocity(b2Vec2(0,0));
_cue->getBody()->SetAngularVelocity(0.0);
_touch = touch;
```

We once again have a `LineContainer` node so we can draw a dashed line between the cue and the spot on the ball where the cue will hit. This serves as a visual aid for the player to prepare his or her shot. The visual aid effect is demonstrated here:

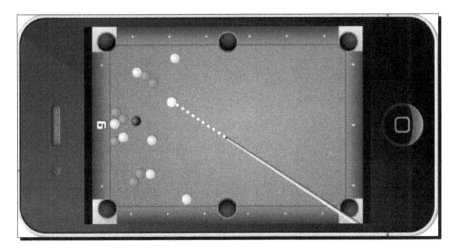

6. In onTouchMoved, we only need to move the cue body based on the position of the player's finger. So we calculate the distance between the moving touch and the white ball. If the cue body is still too close to the ball, we set its body object to sleep and its texture object to invisible.

```
void GameLayer::onTouchMoved(Touch * touch, Event * event) {
    if (touch && touch == _touch) {
        Point tap = touch->getLocation();
        float diffx = tap.x - _player->getPositionX();
        float diffy = tap.y - _player->getPositionY();
        if (pow(diffx,2) + pow(diffy,2) < pow(BALL_RADIUS * 2,2))
{

            _usingCue = false;
            _lineContainer->setDrawing(false);
            _cue->setVisible(false);
            _cue->getBody()->SetAwake(false);
        } else {
            _usingCue = true;
            _cue->setVisible(true);
            _lineContainer->setDrawing(true);
           placeCue(tap);
            _cue->getBody()->SetAwake(true);
        }

    }
}
```

7. Otherwise, we awaken the body and call the placeCue method as follows:

```
void GameLayer::placeCue(Point position) {
    float diffx = _cueStartPoint.x - position.x;
    float diffy = _cueStartPoint.y - position.y;

    float angle = atan2(diffy, diffx);
   float distance = sqrt(pow (diffx, 2) + pow(diffy, 2));

    _pullBack = distance * 0.5f;
    Point cuePosition = Vec2(
        _cueStartPoint.x - (BALL_RADIUS * 21 + _pullBack) *
        cos(angle),
        _cueStartPoint.y - (BALL_RADIUS * 21 + _pullBack) *
        sin(angle)
    );
```

```
        _cue->getBody()->SetTransform(
            b2Vec2(cuePosition.x/PTM_RATIO,
            cuePosition.y/PTM_RATIO),
            angle);

        _lineContainer->setCuePoint(Vec2(
            _cueStartPoint.x - ( _pullBack) * cos(angle),
        _cueStartPoint.y - ( _pullBack) * sin(angle)));
    }
```

This method then calculates the angle and position of the cue body and transforms the cue's b2Body method accordingly. The SetTransform option of a b2Body method takes care of both its position and angle.

8. Finally, in onTouchEnded, we let go of the cue body as follows:

```
void GameLayer::onTouchEnded(Touch* touch, Event* event) {

    if (_usingCue && _touch) {
        auto cueBody = _cue->getBody();
        float angle = cueBody->GetAngle();

        //release cue!
        cueBody->ApplyLinearImpulse(
            b2Vec2 (_pullBack * cos(angle) * SHOT_POWER,
            _pullBack * sin(angle) * SHOT_POWER),
            cueBody->GetWorldCenter());
    }

    _usingCue = false;
    _touch = nullptr;
    _lineContainer->setDrawing(false);
}
```

We use ApplyLinearImpulse. This method receives a vector for the impulse to be applied and the position on the body where this impulse should be applied.

The _pullback variable stores the information of how far the cue body was from the ball when the player released the cue body. The farther it was, the strongest the shot will be.

What just happened?

We added the `touch` events that allow the player to hit the white ball with the cue body. The process is a very simple one. We first need to make sure the player is touching the white ball; then we move the cue body as the player drags his or her finger. Finally, when the touch is released, we make the cue spring towards the white ball with `ApplyLinearImpulse`.

We may also move a body in Box2D by using `SetLinearVelocity` or `ApplyForce`, each with subtle and not-so-subtle differences. I recommend that you play around with these.

The main loop

As I showed you before, the simulation only requires that you call its `Step()` method inside the main loop. Box2D takes care of all of its side of the bargain.

What remains usually is the rest of the game logic: scoring, game states, and updating your sprites to match the `b2Bodies` method.

It's important to call the `update` method of each ball and cue. This is what our `b2Sprite` `update` method looks like:

```
void b2Sprite::update(float dt) {
    if (_body && this->isVisible()) {
        this->setPositionX(_body->GetPosition().x * PTM_RATIO);
        this->setPositionY(_body->GetPosition().y * PTM_RATIO);
        this->setRotation(_RADIANS_TO_DEGREES(-1 * _body-
>GetAngle())));
    }
}
```

All you need to do is make sure the `Sprite` method matches the information in the `b2Body` object. And make sure that you convert meters back to pixels when you do so.

So let's add our main loop.

Time for action – adding the main loop

It's inside our main loop that we update our `b2World` object.

1. Start by updating the simulation as follows:
    ```
    void GameLayer::update(float dt) {

        if (!_running) return;
        if (_gameState == kGameOver) return;
        _world->Step(dt, 10, 10);
    ```

2. Next, we need to determine if the game has finished by checking on the number of balls currently in play. We use the following for that:

```
//track invisible objects
for (auto ball : _balls) {
    if (!ball->isVisible() && ball->getInPlay()) {
        ball->setInPlay(false);
        ball->hide();
        //count down balls
        _ballsInPlay--;
        SimpleAudioEngine::getInstance()-
        >playEffect("drop.wav");
        if (_ballsInPlay == 0) {
            _gameState = kGameOver;
            _gameOver->setVisible(true);
        }
    } else {
        ball->update(dt);
    }
}
```

3. Next, we continue to update the sprites as follows:

```
if (!_cue->isVisible())  {
    _cue->hide();
} else {
    _cue->update(dt);
}
if (!_player->isVisible()) {
    _player->reset();
    _player->setVisible(true);
    SimpleAudioEngine::getInstance()-
    >playEffect("whitedrop.wav");
}
_player->update(dt);
```

4. And we also determine when it's time to allow the player a new shot. I decided to only let that happen if the white ball has stopped. And the quickest way to determine that is to check on its vector. Here's how:

```
//check to see if player ball is slow enough for a new shot
if (_player->mag() < 0.5f && !_canShoot) {
    _player->getBody()->SetLinearVelocity(b2Vec2_zero);
    _player->getBody()->SetAngularVelocity(0);
    _canShoot = true;
}
```

What just happened?

We added our main loop. This will update the Box2D simulation and then it's up to us to take care of positioning our sprites based on the resulting information.

One very important aspect of Box2D is understanding what can be changed inside a `b2World::Step` call and what can't.

For instance, a body cannot be made inactive (`b2Body::SetActive`) or be destroyed (`b2World::DestroyBody`) inside a step. You will need to check on conditions outside the step to make these changes. For instance, in our game, we check to see if the ball sprites are visible or not, and if not then we set their bodies as inactive. And all this is done *after* the call to `b2World::Step`.

Adding a timer to our game

In MiniPool, we count the number of seconds it takes the player to clear the table. Let me show you how to do that.

Time for action – creating a timer

We create timers in pretty much the same way we create our main loop.

1. First, we add a second scheduled event by adding this line to our GameLayer constructor:

   ```
   this->schedule(CC_SCHEDULE_SELECTOR(GameLayer::ticktock), 1.5f);
   ```

2. With this, we create a separate timer that will run the `ticktock` method every `1.5` seconds (I decided in the end that `1.5` seconds looked better).

3. The method keeps updating the value of the `_time` property and displaying it in the `_timer` label.

   ```
   void GameLayer::ticktock(float dt) {
       if ( _gameState == kGamePlay) {
           _time++;
           _timer->setString(std::to_string(_time));
       }
   }
   ```

What just happened?

We added a timer to our game by scheduling a second update—specifying the time interval we wanted—using the `schedule` method.

If you wish to remove a timer, all you need to do is call the `unschedule(SEL_SCHEDULE selector)` method of nodes anywhere in your class.

Now, let's take our Box2D game to Android.

Time for action – running the game in Android

Follow these steps to deploy a Box2D game to Android:

1. Open the `Android.mk` file in a text editor (you'll find it in the folder `proj.android/jni`).

2. Edit the lines in `LOCAL_SRC_FILES` to read:

```
LOCAL_SRC_FILES := hellocpp/main.cpp \
                   ../../Classes/AppDelegate.cpp \
               ../../Classes/GLES-Render.cpp \
               ../../Classes/b2Sprite.cpp \
               ../../Classes/Ball.cpp \
               ../../Classes/CollisionListener.cpp \
               ../../Classes/Cue.cpp \
               ../../Classes/LineContainer.cpp \
               ../../Classes/GameLayer.cpp
```

3. Open the manifest file and set the app orientation to `portrait`.

4. Import the game into Eclipse and wait till all classes are compiled.

5. Build and run your application.

What just happened?

That was it. There is no difference between building a game that uses Box2D and one that does not. The Box2D API is already included in the `make` file, in the line where the classes in the external folder are imported.

And, of course, you don't need to add the `GLES-Render` class in your final project.

Have a go hero

A few changes to make gameplay more interesting could be: add a limit to the number of times the white ball can hit a pocket; and another option is to have the timer work as a countdown one, so the player has a limited time to clear the table before time runs out.

Also, this game could do with a few animations. An `Action` method to scale down and fade out a ball when it hits a pocket would look very nice.

Pop quiz

Q1. What is the main object in a Box2D simulation?

1. `b2Universe`.
2. `b2d`.
3. `b2World`.
4. `b2Simulation`.

Q2. A `b2Body` object can be of which type?

1. `b2_dynamicBody`, `b2_sensorBody`, `b2_liquidBody`.
2. `b2_dynamicBody`, `b2_staticBody`, `b2_kinematicBody`.
3. `b2_staticBody`, `b2_kinematicBody`, `b2_debugBody`.
4. `b2_kinematicBody`, `b2_transparentBody`, `b2_floatingBody`.

Q3. Which of the following list of properties can be set in a fixture definition?

1. Density, friction, restitution, shape.
2. Position, density, bullet state.
3. Angular damping, active state, friction.
4. Linear damping, restitution, fixed rotation.

Q4. If two bodies have the same unique value for their `maskBits` property in their fixture definition, this means:

1. The two bodies can never collide.
2. The two bodies will only trigger begin contact events.
3. The two bodies can only collide with each other.
4. The two bodies will only trigger end contact events.

Summary

Nowadays, it seems like everybody in the world has played or will play a physics-based game at some point in their lives. Box2D is by far the most popular engine in the casual games arena. The commands you learned here can be found in pretty much every port of the engine, including a JavaScript one that is growing in popularity as we speak.

Setting up the engine and getting it up and running is remarkably simple—perhaps too much so. A lot of testing and value tweaking goes into developing a Box2D game and pretty soon you learn that keeping the engine performing as you wish is the most important skill to master when developing physics-based games. Picking the right values for friction, density, restitution, damping, time step, PTM ratio, and so on can make or break your game.

In the next chapter, we'll continue to use Box2D, but we'll focus on what else Cocos2d-x can do to help us organize our games.

9
On the Level – Eskimo

In our next game, we'll go over some important features most games require, but which are not directly related to gameplay. So we'll step over the architecture side of things and talk about reading and writing data, using scene transitions, and creating custom events that your whole application can listen to.

But, of course, I'll add a few gameplay ideas as well!

This time, you'll learn how to:

◆ Create scene transitions

◆ Load external data

◆ Save data using `UserDefault`

◆ Create your own game events with the dispatcher

◆ Use the accelerometer

◆ Reuse Box2D bodies

The game – Eskimo

Little Eskimo boy is late for supper. It is your mission, should you choose to accept it, to guide the little fella back to his igloo.

This is a Box2D game, and the controls are very simple. Tilt the device and the Eskimo will move. If you tap the screen, the Eskimo switches shape between a snow ball and a block of ice, each shape with its own physical characteristics and degrees of maneuverability. The ball has a higher friction, for instance, and the block of ice has none.

And the only way the Eskimo may reach his destination is by hitting the gravity switches spread out all over the screen.

Eskimo combines elements from an arcade game with elements of a puzzle game, as each level was planned with one perfect solution in mind as to how to take the little Eskimo home. Note, however, that multiple solutions are possible.

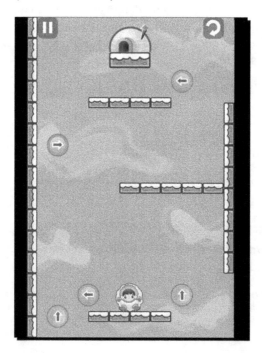

Download the `4198_09_FINAL_PROJECT.zip` file and run the game when you have a chance. Once again, there is no need for extraneous typing as the logic used in the game is pretty much old news to you, and we'll go over the new bits in depth.

The game settings

This is a portrait-only game and accelerometer-based, so it should not autorotate. It was designed for the regular iPhone and its screen resolution size is set to `kResolutionShowAll`, so the screen settings are similar to the ones in our previous game.

Designing a game for the iPhone screen and using the `kResolutionShowAll` parameter will result in the so-called **letterbox** view when playing the game in screens that do not match the iPhone's 1.5 ratio. This means you see borders around the game screen. Alternatively, you could use the `kResolutionNoBorders` parameter, which results in a **zoom-in** effect, causing the game to play at full screen but the areas around the borders will be cropped.

The following screenshot illustrates these two cases:

The one on the left is the game screen on the iPad, using `kResolutionShowAll`. The one on the right uses `kResolutionNoBorders`. Note how the screen is zoomed in and cropped on the second one. When using `kResolutionNoBorders`, it's important to design your game so that no vital gameplay element appears too close to the borders as it may not be displayed.

Organizing the game

Once again, there is a b2Sprite class, and the Eskimo and Platform classes extend b2Sprite. Then there are the regular Sprite classes, GSwitch (which stands for gravity switch) and Igloo. The logic runs collision detection between these last two and Eskimo, but I chose not to have them as sensor bodies because I wanted to show you that 2D collision logic for the Cocos2d-x elements can coexist with collision logic for the Box2D elements just fine.

But most importantly, this game now has three scenes. So far in this book, we've only used one scene per game. This game's scene objects will wrap MenuLayer, LevelSelectLayer, and GameLayer. Here's a brief note on all three:

- In MenuLayer, you have the option to play the game, which will take you to LevelSelectLayer or to play a tutorial for the game, which will take you to GameLayer.

- In LevelSelectLayer, you may choose which available level you want to play, and that will take you to GameLayer. Or you may go back to MenuLayer.

- In GameLayer, you play the game, and may go back to MenuLayer upon game over.

The following image illustrates all three scenes in the game:

Using scenes in Cocos2d-x

Scenes are mini applications themselves. If you have experience as an Android developer, you may think of scenes as activities. Of all the classes based on node, the `Scene` application is the most architecturally relevant, because the `Director` class runs a scene, in effect running your application.

Part of the benefit of working with scenes is also part of the drawback: they are wholly independent and ignorant of each other. The need to share information between scenes will be a major factor when planning your game class structure.

Also, memory management may become an issue. A currently running scene will not give up its ghost until a new scene is up and running. So, when you use transition animations, keep in mind that for a few seconds, both scenes will exist in memory.

In Eskimo, I initialize scenes in two different ways. With `MenuLayer` and `LevelSelectLayer`, each time the user navigates to either one of these scenes, a new layer object is created (either a new `MenuLayer` or a new `LevelSelectLayer`).

`GameLayer`, however, is different. It is a singleton `Layer` class that never stays out of memory after its first instantiation, therefore speeding up the time from level selection to the actual playing. This may not work for every game, however. As I mentioned earlier, when transitioning between scenes, both scenes stay in memory for a few seconds. But here we are adding to that problem by keeping one layer in memory the whole time. Eskimo, however, is not very big memory-wise. Note that we could still have the option of creating special conditions for when `GameLayer` should be destroyed, and conditions when it should not.

So let me show you how to create scene transitions. First, with a `Scene` class that creates a fresh copy of its `Layer` each time it's created.

Time for action – creating a scene transition

You have, of course, been using scenes all along.

1. Hidden in `AppDelegate.cpp`, you've had lines like:
```
auto scene = GameLayer::scene();
// run
director->runWithScene(scene);
```

2. So, in order to change scenes, all you need to do is tell the `Director` class which scene you wish it to run. Cocos2d-x will then get rid of all the content in the current scene, if any (all their destructors will be called), and a new layer will be instantiated and wrapped inside the new `Scene`.

3. Breaking the steps down a little further, this is how you usually create a new scene for `Director`:

```
Scene* MenuLayer::scene()
{
    // 'scene' is an autorelease object
    auto scene = Scene::create();
    // add layer as a child to scene
    auto layer = new MenuLayer();
    scene->addChild(layer);
    layer->release();
    return scene;
}
```

4. The static `MenuLayer::scene` method will create a blank scene, and then create a new instance of `MenuLayer` and add it as a child to the new scene.

5. Now you can tell `Director` to run it as follows:

```
Director::getInstance()->replaceScene(MenuLayer::scene());
```

6. The logic changes a little if you wish to use a transition effect. So, inside our `MenuLayer.cpp` class, this is how we transition to `LevelSelectLayer`:

```
auto newScene = TransitionMoveInR::create(0.2f,
LevelSelectLayer::scene());
Director::getInstance()->replaceScene(newScene);
```

The code just described creates a new transition object that will slide in the new scene from the right-hand side of the screen to lie on top of the current one. The transition will take `0.2` seconds.

What just happened?

You created a scene transition animation with Cocos2d-x.

As I mentioned earlier, this form of scene change will cause a new instance of the new layer to be created each time, and destroyed each time it's replaced by a new scene. So, in our game, `MenuLayer` and `LevelSelectLayer` are instantiated and destroyed as many times as the user switches between them.

There is also the option to use `pushScene` instead of `replaceScene`. This creates a stack of `scene` objects and keeps them all in memory. This stack can be navigated with `popScene` and `popToRootScene`.

Now let me show you how to do the same thing but with a singleton layer.

It should be no surprise to you by now that you will find many examples of these transition classes in the `Tests`, project at `tests/cpp-tests/Classes/TransitionsTest`.

Time for action – creating transitions with a singleton Layer class

We first need to make sure the layer in question can only be instantiated once.

1. The `scene` static method in `GameLayer` looks like this:

```
Scene* GameLayer::scene(int level, int levelsCompleted)
{
    // 'scene' is an autorelease object
    auto scene = Scene::create();
    // add layer as a child to scene
    scene->addChild(GameLayer::create(level, levelsCompleted));
    return scene;
}
```

This layer receives two parameters when created: the game level it should load and the number of levels completed by the player. We create a new `Scene` object and add `GameLayer` as its child.

2. But take a look at the static `create` method in `GameLayer`:

```
GameLayer * GameLayer::create (int level, int levelsCompleted) {
    if (!_instance) {
        _instance = new GameLayer();
    } else {
        _instance->clearLayer();
    }
    _instance->setLevelsCompleted(levelsCompleted);
    _instance->loadLevel(level);
    _instance->scheduleUpdate();
    return _instance;
}
```

3. An `_instance` static property is declared at the top of `GameLayer.cpp` as follows:

```
static GameLayer* _instance = nullptr;
```

We can check, then, if the one instance of `GameLayer` is currently in memory and instantiate it if necessary.

4. The scene transition to `GameLayer` will look, on the surface, to be exactly like the regular kind of transition. So, in `LevelSelectLayer`, we have the following:

```
auto newScene = TransitionMoveInR::create(0.2f,
GameLayer::scene(_firstIndex + i, _levelsCompleted));
Director::sharedDirector()->replaceScene(newScene);
```

What just happened?

We have created a `Scene` transition with a `Layer` class that never gets destroyed, so we don't have to instantiate new platform and gravity switch sprites with each new level.

There are, of course, problems and limitations with this process. We cannot transition between the two `GameLayer` objects, for instance, as we only ever have one of these objects.

There are also some special considerations when leaving `GameLayer` and when getting back to it. For instance, we must make sure we have our main loop running when we get back to `GameLayer`.

The only way to do that is by unscheduling it whenever leaving `GameLayer` and scheduling it again when returning, as follows:

```
//when leaving
unscheduleUpdate();
auto newScene = TransitionMoveInL::create(0.2f, MenuLayer::scene());
Director::sharedDirector()->replaceScene(newScene);

//when returning
_instance->scheduleUpdate();
```

Again, architecturally speaking, there are even better options. Possibly the best one is creating your own game elements cache, or game manager, with object pools and everything that needs instantiating stored inside it. And then have this cache be a singleton that every scene can access. This is also the best way to share game-relevant data between scenes.

Loading external data from a .plist file

Eskimo has only five game levels, plus a tutorial level (feel free to add more). The data for these levels exist inside a `levels.plist` file, stored inside the `Resources` folder. A `.plist` file is an XML-formatted data file, and as such can be created in any text editor. Xcode, however, offers a nice GUI to edit the files.

Let me show you how to create them inside Xcode.

Time for action – creating a .plist file

You could, of course, create this in any text editor, but Xcode makes it extra easy to create and edit .plist files.

1. Inside Xcode, go to **New** | **File...** and then select **Resource** and **Property List**. When asked where to save the file, choose any location you want.

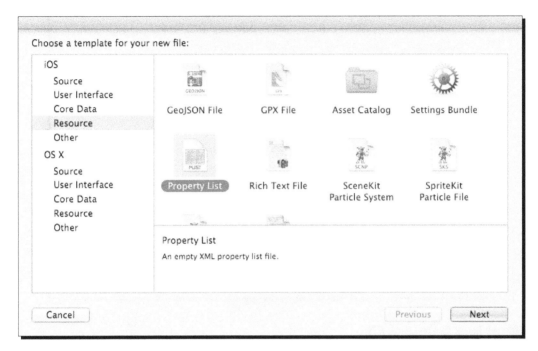

2. You need to decide what the **Root** element of your .plist file will be—either an **Array** or a **Dictionary** (the default) type. For Eskimo, the **Root** element is **Array** containing a series of dictionaries, each holding the data for a level in the game.

3. By selecting the **Root** element, you get a plus sign indicator right next to the **Type** declaration. Clicking on this plus sign will add an element to **Root**. You can then pick the data type for this new item. The options are **Boolean**, **Data**, **Date**, **Number**, **String**, and again **Array** and **Dictionary**. The last two can contain subitems in the tree, just like the **Root** element.

4. Keep adding elements to the tree, trying to match the items in the following screenshot:

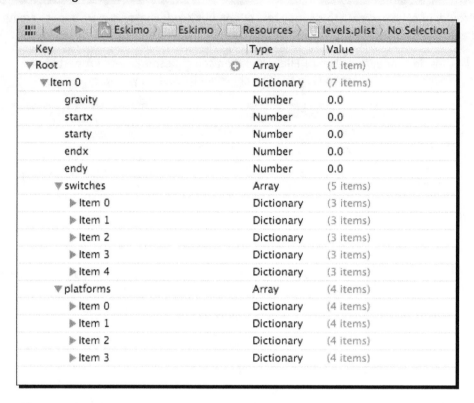

What just happened?

You just created a property list file in Xcode. This is XML-structured data that Cocos2d-x can load and parse. You've used them already when loading particles and sprite sheet information.

Loading the level data

In Eskimo, since I only have five levels, I chose to have one `.plist` file that contains all levels. This may not be the best option in a larger game.

Although Apple devices will load and parse the `.plist` files quickly, the same may not be true for other targets. So limit the size of your `.plist` files by organizing the data into multiple files. You've probably seen games that divide their levels into multiple groups or packs. This is a simple way to create an extra preloading screen your game can use to parse level data. This can also be used as a means to keep file sizes to a minimum.

In Eskimo, we could have the `.plist` files containing 10 levels each, for instance, and then 10 groups of these, totaling 100 levels.

So it's time to load our `.plist` file and parse the data for our levels.

Time for action – retrieving data from the .plist file

The level data is loaded in `GameLayer`.

1. Inside the `GameLayer` constructor, we load the data like this:

```
_levels = FileUtils::getInstance()-
>getValueVectorFromFile("levels.plist");
```

Cocos2d-x will take care of mapping `FileUtils` to the correct target. There is `FileUtils` for each platform that is supported by the framework and they all can be made to work with the `.plist` format. Sweet! If the data in the `.plist` file is an **Array**, you must convert it to `ValueVector`; if it's **Dictionary**, you must convert it to a `ValueMap`. We'll do that next when we load the data for a specific level.

 If we divide the levels into multiple `.plist` files, then we would need logic to refresh the `_levels` array each time a new `.plist` file is loaded.

2. Inside the `loadLevel` method, we load the data for the level like this:

```
ValueMap levelData = _levels.at(_currentLevel).asValueMap();
```

Here, the data in the `.plist` file is **Dictionary**, so we must convert the data into a `ValueMap`.

And that's it for the loading and parsing. Now we can proceed to retrieving data for our level.

Each level dictionary starts with the data regarding the level's gravity (a level may start with a different gravity value), the start point where the player should be placed, and the end point where the igloo should be placed.

3. These values are retrieved like this in our code:

```
_gravity = levelData.at("gravity").asInt();
switch (_gravity) {
    case kDirectionUp:
        _world->SetGravity(b2Vec2(0,FORCE_GRAVITY));
        break;
    case kDirectionDown:
        _world->SetGravity(b2Vec2(0,-FORCE_GRAVITY));
        break;
```

```
        case kDirectionLeft:
            _world->SetGravity(b2Vec2(-FORCE_GRAVITY, 0));
            break;
        case kDirectionRight:
            _world->SetGravity(b2Vec2(FORCE_GRAVITY, 0));
            break;
    }

    _player->setSpritePosition(Vec2(
        levelData.at("startx").asFloat() * TILE,
        levelData.at("starty").asFloat() * TILE
    ));

    _igloo->initIgloo(_gravity, Vec2(
        levelData.at("endx").asFloat() * TILE,
        levelData.at("endy").asFloat() * TILE
    ));
```

4. Inside this same dictionary, we have an array for platforms and an array for gravity switches. These are retrieved like this:

```
ValueVector platforms =
levelData.at("platforms").asValueVector();
ValueVector switches =
levelData.at("switches").asValueVector();
```

5. These arrays contain even more dictionaries containing data for the creation and placement of platforms and gravity switches in each level. This data is passed to the corresponding `Platform` and `GSwitch` classes, and boom—you've got yourself a level.

```
for ( auto platformData : platforms){
    ValueMap data = platformData.asValueMap();
    platform->initPlatform ( data.at("width").asInt() * TILE,
                            data.at("angle").asFloat(),
                            Vec2(data.at("x").asFloat() * TILE,
                            data.at("y").asFloat() * TILE));
}

  for (int i = 0; i < switches.size(); i++) {
        auto gswitch = _gSwitchPool.at(i);
        ValueMap data = switches.at(i).asValueMap();
        gswitch->initGSwitch(data.at("gravity").asInt(),
                    Vec2(data.at("x").asFloat() * TILE,
                    data.at("y").asFloat() * TILE));
}
```

What just happened?

Parsing and retrieving data from a property list file is a breeze with Cocos2d-x. You will always work with either an array of values or a dictionary of values and map these to a `ValueVector` or `ValueMap` respectively.

Saving game data

When planning your games, you may soon decide you wish to store data related to your application, such as highest score or user preferences. In Cocos2d-x, you can do this by simply accessing the `UserDefault` singleton.

With `UserDefault`, you can store integers, floats, doubles, strings, and Boolean with just one simple call per each data type, as follows:

```
UserDefault::getInstance()->setIntegerForKey("levelsCompleted", _
levelsCompleted);
UserDefault::getInstance()->flush();
```

The other methods are `setFloatForKey`, `setDoubleForKey`, `setStringForKey`, and `setBoolForKey`. To retrieve data, you use their respective getters.

I'll show you next how to use that in our game.

Time for action – storing the completed levels

Open the `LevelSelectLayer` class.

1. This is how the number of levels completed is retrieved from inside the layer's constructor:

    ```
    _levelsCompleted = UserDefault::getInstance()-
    >getIntegerForKey("levelsCompleted");
    ```

2. Initially, `_levelsCompleted` will equal 0 if no data is present. So we store level 1 as "unlocked". This is how that's done:

    ```
    if (_levelsCompleted == 0) {
        _levelsCompleted = 1;
        UserDefault::getInstance()->setIntegerForKey("levelsComplet
    ed", 1);
        UserDefault::getInstance()->flush();
    }
    ```

3. Then, whenever we start a new level, we update the number of levels completed if the new level number is larger than the value stored.

```
if (_currentLevel > _levelsCompleted) {
    _levelsCompleted = _currentLevel;
    UserDefault::getInstance()->setIntegerForKey("levelsComplet
ed", _levelsCompleted);
    UserDefault::getInstance()->flush();
}
```

> You don't have to flush the data (using `flush`) each time you update every single bit in it. You can group multiple updates under one flush, or find a spot in your logic where you can safely flush updates before exiting the app. Nodes come with extremely helpful methods for this: `onEnter`, `onExit`, `onEnterTransitionDidFinish`, and `onExitTransitionDidStart`.

What just happened?

For small bits of data related to your game, settings, and preferences, `UserDefault` is an excellent way to store information. Cocos2d-x once again will map this to whatever local storage is available in each target system.

Using events in your game

Earlier versions of the framework used an Objective-C-inspired feature of notifications. But this particular API is already on its way to being deprecated. Instead, you should use the all-knowing `Director` and its `Dispatcher` (the same object we've been talking to when listening to touch events).

If you have ever worked with an MVC framework or developed a game AI system, you are probably familiar with a design pattern called the **Observer Pattern**. This consists of a central message dispatcher object other objects can subscribe to (observe) in order to listen to special messages, or order it to dispatch their own messages to other subscribers. In other words, it's an event model.

With Cocos2d-x, this is done very quickly and easily. Let me give you an example used in Eskimo.

Time for action – using the event dispatcher

If we want the `Platform` sprite to listen to the special notification `NOTIFICATION_GRAVITY_SWITCH`, all we need to do is add `Platform` as an observer.

1. Inside the `Platform` class, in its constructor, you will find these lines:

```
auto onGravityChanged = [=] (EventCustom * event) {
        if (this->isVisible()) {
            switchTexture();
        }
};
Director::getInstance()->getEventDispatcher()-
addEventListenerWithSceneGraphPriority(EventListenerCustom::create
(GameLayer::NOTIFICATION_GRAVITY_SWITCH, onGravityChanged), this);
```

And yes, it is one line of code! It is best to create a macro for both the dispatcher and the add listener code; so, something like this:

```
#define EVENT_DISPATCHER Director::getInstance()-
>getEventDispatcher()
#define ADD_NOTIFICATION( __target__, __notification__,
__handler__) EVENT_DISPATCHER-
addEventListenerWithSceneGraphPriority(EventListenerCustom::create
(__notification__, __handler__), __target__);
```

This way the same line of code we used before would look like this:

```
ADD_NOTIFICATION(this, GameLayer::NOTIFICATION_GRAVITY_SWITCH,
onGravityChanged);
```

2. The message (or notification), `NOTIFICATION_GRAVITY_SWITCH`, is created as a static string in `GameLayer`:

```
const char* GameLayer::NOTIFICATION_GRAVITY_SWITCH =
"NOTIFICATION_GRAVITY_SWITCH";
```

The one-line call to the `Director` class's dispatcher tells it that the `Platform` objects will listen to this defined message, and when such a message is dispatched, every `Platform` object will call the `onGravityChanged` method. This method does not need to be a block as I showed here, but it is more readable to have the handler appear as close to the `Add Listener` call as possible. So, simple blocks are a good way to organize listeners and their handlers.

3. In the game, each gravity switch is color coded, and when the Eskimo hits a switch, the platform's texture changes to reflect the new gravity by switching to the color of the activated gravity switch. This is all done through a simple notification we dispatch inside `GameLayer` when a collision with a `GSwitch` object is detected inside the main loop. This is how we do that:

```
Director::getInstance()->getEventDispatcher()-
>dispatchCustomEvent( GameLayer::NOTIFICATION_GRAVITY_SWITCH);
```

Or, if you are using the macro, use this:

```
EVENT_DISPATCHER->dispatchCustomEvent(
GameLayer::NOTIFICATION_GRAVITY_SWITCH);
```

4. You can also add a `UserData` object in the custom event as a second parameter in the dispatch. This can be retrieved from the `EventCustom *` event in the event handler, like this:

```
event->getUserData();
```

5. When `Platform` objects are destroyed, the `Node` destructor will take care of removing the node as a listener.

What just happened?

You have just learned how to make your life as a developer much, much easier. Adding an application-wide event model to your game is such a powerful way to improve flow and interactivity between objects and it's so simple to use that I'm sure you'll soon implement this feature in all your games.

Using the accelerometer

Now let's move to the few new topics related to gameplay, the first of which is the use of accelerometer data. Again, nothing could be simpler.

Time for action – reading accelerometer data

Just as you do with `touch` events, you need to tell the framework you want to read accelerometer data.

1. You tell the framework you wish to use the accelerometer with this one call inside any `Layer` class:

```
Device::setAccelerometerEnabled(true);
```

2. Then, just as you've done with `touch` events, you subscribe to the `accelerometer` events from the event dispatcher as follows:

```
auto listenerAccelerometer =
EventListenerAcceleration::create(CC_CALLBACK_2
(GameLayer::onAcceleration, this));
_eventDispatcher->addEventListenerWithSceneGraphPriority(listenerA
ccelerometer,
this);
```

3. In Eskimo, the accelerometer data changes the value of a `Point` vector called `_acceleration`.

```
void GameLayer::onAcceleration(Acceleration *acc, Event *event) {
    _acceleration = Vec2(acc->x * ACCELEROMETER_MULTIPLIER,
                         acc->y * ACCELEROMETER_MULTIPLIER);
}
```

This value is then read inside the main loop and used to move the Eskimo. In the game, only one axis is updated at a time, depending on the current gravity. So you can only ever move the Eskimo on the X axis or the Y axis with the accelerometer data, but never both at the same time.

 Keep in mind that there is also a Z axis value in the `Acceleration` data. It might come in handy someday!

What just happened?

Yep. With a couple of lines, you added accelerometer controls to your game.

It is common practice to add extra filters to these accelerometer values, as results may vary between devices. These filters are ratios you apply to acceleration to keep values within a certain range. You can also find a variety of formulas for these ratios online. But these will depend on how sensitive you need the controls to be or how responsive.

And, in the game, we only update the Eskimo with the accelerometer data if the sprite is touching a platform. We can quickly ascertain that by checking whether or not the `_player` body has a contact list, as follows:

```
if (_player->getBody()->GetContactList())
```

Reusing b2Bodies

In Eskimo, we have a pool of b2Bodies that are used inside the Platform objects and we also change the shape of the little Eskimo whenever the player taps the screen. This is possible because Box2D makes it very easy to change the fixture data of a b2Body fixture without having to destroy the actual body.

Let me show you how.

Time for action – changing a b2Body fixture

All you have to do is make a call to body->DestroyFixture. Not surprisingly, this should be done outside the simulation step.

1. Inside the methods makeCircleShape and makeBoxShape in the Eskimo class, you will find these lines:

   ```
   if (_body->GetFixtureList() ) {
       _body->DestroyFixture(_body->GetFixtureList());
   }
   ```

   Here we just state that if there is a fixture for this body, destroy it. We can then switch from a box to a circle fixture when the player taps the screen, but use the same body throughout.

2. We use this feature with platforms too. Platforms inside the pool that are not being used in the current level are set to inactive as follows:

   ```
   _body->SetActive(false);
   ```

   This removes them from the simulation.

3. And when they are reinitialized to be used in a level, we destroy their existing fixture, update it to match the data from the .plist file, and set the body to active once again. This is how we do that:

   ```
   //Define shape
   b2PolygonShape box;
   box.SetAsBox(width * 0.5f /PTM_RATIO, PLATFORM_HEIGHT *
   0.5f / PTM_RATIO);

   //Define fixture
   b2FixtureDef fixtureDef;
   fixtureDef.shape = &box;
   fixtureDef.density = 1;
   ```

```
fixtureDef.restitution = 0;

//reutilize body from the pool: so destroy any existent fixture
if (_body->GetFixtureList()) {
    _body->DestroyFixture(_body->GetFixtureList());
}
_body->CreateFixture(&fixtureDef);
_body->SetTransform(b2Vec2(position.x / PTM_RATIO, position.y /
PTM_RATIO), _DEGREES_TO_RADIANS(-angle));
_body->SetActive(true);
```

What just happened?

So, just as we've been doing with pools of sprites, we can apply the same logic to `b2Bodies` and never instantiate anything inside the main loop.

Now, let's see how Android handles all this level-loading business.

Time for action – running the game in Android

Time to deploy the game to Android.

1. Navigate to the `proj.android` folder and open the file `AndroidManifest.xml` in a text editor. Then go to the folder `jni` and open the file `Android.mk` in a text editor.

2. In the `AndroidManifest.xml` file, edit the following line in the `activity` tag as follows:

    ```
    android:screenOrientation="portrait"
    ```

3. Next, let's edit the make file, so open the `Android.mk` file and edit the lines in `LOCAL_SRC_FILES` to read:

    ```
    LOCAL_SRC_FILES := hellocpp/main.cpp \
                    ../../Classes/AppDelegate.cpp \
                    ../../Classes/b2Sprite.cpp \
                    ../../Classes/Eskimo.cpp \
                    ../../Classes/GSwitch.cpp \
                    ../../Classes/Igloo.cpp \
                    ../../Classes/Platform.cpp \
                    ../../Classes/LevelSelectLayer.cpp \
                    ../../Classes/MenuLayer.cpp \
                    ../../Classes/GameLayer.cpp
    ```

4. Now import the project into Eclipse and build it.

5. You can now save it and run the game in your Android device.

What just happened?

By now, you should be an expert at running your code in Android and hopefully your experience with Eclipse has been a good one.

And that's all folks!

Play the game. Check out the source code (which is chock-full of comments). Add some new levels and make the little Eskimo's life a living hell!

Have a go hero

The gameplay for Eskimo could be further improved with a few new ideas that would force the player to make more errors.

It is a common feature in these types of games to evaluate the degree of "completeness" in which a level was played. There could be a time limit for each level and pick-up items for the Eskimo, and the player could be evaluated at the end of each level and awarded a bronze, silver, or golden star based on his or her performance. And new groups of levels may only be unlocked if a certain number of golden stars were acquired.

Summary

Yes, you have a cool idea for a game, great! But a lot of effort will go into structuring and optimizing it. Cocos2d-x can help with both sides of the job.

Yes, scenes can be a bit cumbersome depending on your needs, but they are undisputed memory managers. When `Director` kills a scene, it kills it dead.

Loading external data can not only help with memory size, but also bring in more developers into your project, focusing specifically on level design and the external data files that create them.

And events can quickly become a must in the way you structure your games. Pretty soon, you will find yourself thinking in terms of events to handle game states and menu interactivity, among other things.

Now, let's move to a whole new language!

10
Introducing Lua!

In our last game, we'll move to the new Cocos IDE and develop an entire game using the Lua scripting language. You'll get to know and use the Lua bindings for the Cocos2d-x API, which is not much different from what we've been using in C++; if anything, it's just a lot easier!

This time, you'll learn how to:

◆ Create and publish a project in Cocos IDE

◆ Code an entire game in Lua

◆ Use sprites, particles, labels, menus, and actions, but this time with the Lua bindings

◆ Build a match-three game

So what is Lua like?

At the heart of Lua (which means moon in Portuguese), you have the table. You may think of it as being similar to a JavaScript object, only it's much more than that. It plays the part of arrays, dictionaries, enumerations, structures, and classes, among other things. It makes Lua the perfect language to manage large sets of data. You write a script that handles the data, and then keep feeding it different "stuff." An inventory or shop system, an interactive children's book—these types of projects could all benefit from Lua's table-centric power, as they can be built around a fixed template with a data table at its core.

Its syntax, for those not used to a scripting language, can be a little odd, with its dos, thens, and ends. But once you get past this initial hurdle, you'll find Lua quite user-friendly. Here are some of the "oddities" in its syntax:

```
-- a comment
--[[
a
multiline
comment
]]
-- a table declared as a local variable
local myTable = {}
-- the length of a table
local len = #myTable
-- looping the table (starting with index 1!)
for i = 1, #myTable do
    local element = myTable[i]
    -- an if elseif else statement
    if (element ~= true ) then
        -- do something
    elseif (element == true) then
        -- do something else
    else
        -- we'll never get here!
    end
end
```

 Semicolons are optional.

A table can be turned into a template to generate instances of it, in other words, a class. Methods of the instance of the table must be accessed with a : notation:

```
myTableClassObject:myMethod()
```

From inside the method, you refer to the instance of the class as `self`:

```
self.myProperty = 1
self:myOtherMethod()
```

Alternatively, you can call the template's method with a dot notation, passing the instance of that template to it as the first parameter:

```
myTableClassObject.myMethod(myTableClassObject)
```

I admit, it's weird, but it can be useful at times as pretty much every method you write in Lua can be made available for other parts of your code—sort of the way static methods are used in traditional OOP languages.

Debugging in Lua – the knights who say nil

Debugging your Lua code can be frustrating at times. But you soon learn to distinguish between the minute subtleties in Lua's runtime errors. The compiler will say something is `nil` (Lua's `null`) in about 99.9 percent of cases. It's up to you to figure out why. Here are the main culprits:

- ◆ You are referencing an object's own property without prepending `self.` or `self:`.
- ◆ You are calling an instance method with a dot notation, and not passing the instance as the first parameter; something like `myObject.myMethod()` instead of `myObject.myMethod(myObject)`. Use `myObject:myMethod()` instead.
- ◆ You are referencing a variable from a place outside its scope. For example, a local variable declared inside an `if` statement is being referenced outside the conditional.
- ◆ You forgot to return the class object at the end of your class or module/table declaration.
- ◆ You tried to access the zero index of an array.
- ◆ You forgot to add a few dos and thens or ends.
- ◆ And finally, maybe you're just having one of those days. A `nil` sort of day.

The Cocos IDE will show errors in bold; the same bold it uses for global variables, which is confusing at times. But it helps nonetheless. Just make a habit of scanning your code for bold text!

> You might need to increase the heap memory inside the IDE. The quickest way to accomplish this is to find the file called `eclipse.ini` inside the Cocos IDE application folder. On a Mac, this means inside the Cocos IDE app package: right-click on the app icon, select **Show Package Contents**, and then navigate to **Contents/MacOS/eclipse.ini**.
>
> Then find the line where you read `-Xmx256m` or `-Xmx512m` and change it to `-Xmx1024m`.
>
> This might help in slower computers. My laptop crashed a lot while running the IDE.

The game – Stone Age

This is a match-three game. You know, the kind of game that is making a couple of companies a gazillion dollars and making a gazillion other companies clone those games in order to earn a couple of dollars. Yes, that game!

You must match three or more gems. If you match more than three, a random gem bursts and turns into a diamond, which you collect for more points.

The game has a timer, and when time runs out, it's game over.

I used pretty much the same structure as in the previous games in this book. But I broke it into separate modules so it's easier for you to use the code as a reference.

We have a `MenuScene` and a `GameScene` item. I have pretty much all Cocos2d-x actions in one module called `GridAnimations` and most of the interactivity inside another module called `GridController`. And all object pools are kept inside a class called `ObjectPools`.

This is a grid game, so it's perfect to illustrate working with table arrays in Lua, and its main advantages over C++: it's much easier to create and memory manage dynamic lists (arrays) in Lua. This flexibility, aligned with Cocos2d-x's awesomeness, make for very rapid prototyping and development. The actual game will look like this:

But before you import the starter project, let me show you how to create a new project inside the Cocos IDE.

Time for action – creating or importing a project

Nothing could be simpler; since the IDE is based on Eclipse, you know most of its main functionalities already:

1. First let's set up the IDE to use the Lua bindings. Go to **Preferences | Cocos | Lua**, and in the drop-down menu for **Lua Frameworks**, find the Cocos2d-x framework folder you downloaded:

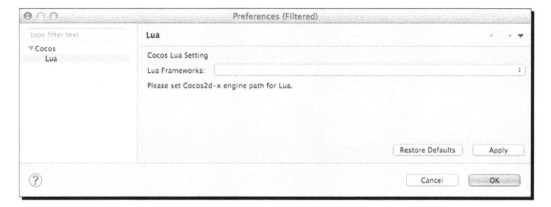

2. Select **File | New | Cocos Lua Project**, if that option is already available, or select **File | New | Other | Cocos Lua | Cocos Lua Project**.

3. In the **New Cocos Project** wizard, give your project a name and click **Next**.

4. In the next dialogue, you can choose your project's orientation and design size. And that's it. Click **Finish**.

5. In order to import a project, click **File | Import** then **Cocos | Import Cocos Project**, and navigate to the project start folder for this chapter. The game is called StoneAge. (Download this chapter's source files from this book's website if you haven't done so already. There is a starter project and a final project that you can run and test.)

What just happened?

You learned to create and import a project into the Cocos IDE. Since the IDE is an Eclipse-based program, the steps should be familiar to you by now.

You may also wish to change the settings for the simulator. For that, all you need to do is right-click on your project and select either **Run As...** or **Debug As...**, and then **Run** or **Debug Configurations**.

It's best to leave the default for the **Mac OSX** runtime (if you're on a Mac of course), as this is the fastest option. But if you wish to change the simulator, here is where you do it:

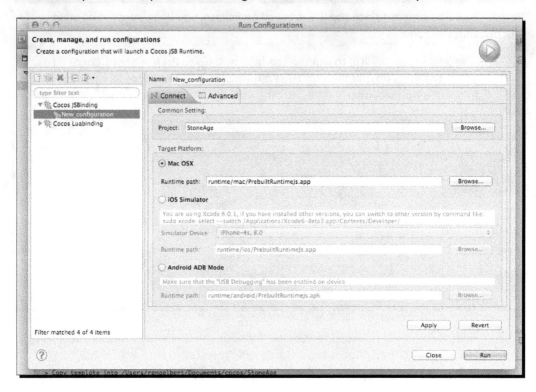

 On my machine, version 3.4 of the framework threw compile errors. I had to add two fixes in order to run Stone Age. In `cocos-cocos2d-Cocos2dConstants.lua`, just before the last table is declared, I added this line:

```
cc.AsyncTaskPool = {}
```

Similarly, in `cocos-ui-GuiConstants.lua`, I added `ccui.LayoutComponent = {}` before new tables are added to `LayoutComponent`, also near the end of the file.

If you run into problems, switch to version 3.3, which was much more stable for Lua development.

Time for action – setting up our screen resolution

The old `AppDelegate` class logic now exists inside a file called `main.lua`:

1. In the IDE, open the `main.lua` file inside the `src` folder.

2. After the line where we set the animation interval, type the following:

```
cc.Director:getInstance():getOpenGLView():
setDesignResolutionSize(640, 960,
cc.ResolutionPolicy.SHOW_ALL)
   local screenSize =
cc.Director:getInstance():getVisibleSize()
   local designSize = cc.size(640, 960)
   if (screenSize.width > 320) then
     cc.Director:getInstance():setContentScaleFactor(640/
designSize.width)
      cc.FileUtils:getInstance():addSearchPath("res/hd/")
   else
      cc.Director:getInstance():setContentScaleFactor(320/
designSize.width)
      cc.FileUtils:getInstance():addSearchPath("res/sd/")
   end
```

3. I designed the game for iPhone retina, and here we set the appropriate scale and asset folder for both retina and non-retina phones. Next, let's preload the sound files:

```
    local bgMusicPath =
cc.FileUtils:getInstance():fullPathForFilename("background.mp3")
      cc.SimpleAudioEngine:getInstance():preloadMusic(bgMusicPa
th)
      local effectPath =
cc.FileUtils:getInstance():fullPathForFilename("match.wav")
      cc.SimpleAudioEngine:getInstance():preloadEffect(effectPa
th)
   effectPath =
cc.FileUtils:getInstance():fullPathForFilename("diamond.wav")
      cc.SimpleAudioEngine:getInstance():preloadEffect(effectPa
th)
      effectPath =
cc.FileUtils:getInstance():fullPathForFilename("diamond2.wav")
      cc.SimpleAudioEngine:getInstance():preloadEffect(effectPa
th)
      effectPath =
cc.FileUtils:getInstance():fullPathForFilename("wrong.wav")
   cc.SimpleAudioEngine:getInstance():preloadEffect(effectPath)
```

4. And finally, let's set the ball rolling by creating and running our first scene:

```
--create scene
local scene = require("MenuScene")
local menuScene = scene.create()
if cc.Director:getInstance():getRunningScene() then
        cc.Director:getInstance():replaceScene(menuScene)
    else
        cc.Director:getInstance():runWithScene(menuScene)
    end
```

What just happened?

Like we've done in pretty much every game so far, we set the resolution policy and scale factor for our application and preloaded the sounds we'll be using.

The game was designed only for phones this time, and it was designed with the iPhone 4 screen in mind, and it resizes to older phones.

But don't run the game just yet. Let's create our menu scene. It has a little of everything in it and it will be a perfect introduction to the Cocos2d-x API in Lua.

Time for action – creating a menu scene

Let's create a new file and add a menu scene to our game:

1. Right-click on the `src` folder and select **New | Lua File**; call the new file `MenuScene.lua`.

2. Let's create a class that extends a scene. We first load our own module of all the game's constants (this file already exists in the starter project):

```
local constants = require ("constants")
```

3. Then we build our class:

```
local MenuScene = class("MenuScene", function()
    return cc.Scene:create()
end)

function MenuScene.create()
    local scene = MenuScene.new()
    return scene
end

function MenuScene:ctor()
```

```
    self.visibleSize =
cc.Director:getInstance():getVisibleSize()
    self.middle = {x = self.visibleSize.width * 0.5,
y = self.visibleSize.height * 0.5}
    self.origin = cc.Director:getInstance():getVisibleOrigin()
    self:init()
end
return MenuScene
```

We'll add the methods next, including the `init` method we called in the class constructor (always called `ctor`), but I wanted to stress the importance of returning the class at the end of its declaration.

4. So moving just below the constructor, let's continue building up our scene:

```
function MenuScene:init ()
    local bg = cc.Sprite:create("introbg.jpg")
    bg:setPosition(self.middle.x, self.middle.y)
    self:addChild(bg)
    --create pterodactyl animation
    local pterodactyl = cc.Sprite:create("ptero_frame1.png")
    pterodactyl:setPosition(cc.p(self.visibleSize.width + 100,
self.visibleSize.height * 0.8))
    self:addChild(pterodactyl)
    local animation = cc.Animation:create()
    local number, name
    for i = 1, 3 do
      number = i
      name = "ptero_frame"..number..".png"
      animation:addSpriteFrameWithFile(name)
    end
    animation:setDelayPerUnit(0.5 / 3.0)
    animation:setRestoreOriginalFrame(true)
    animation:setLoops(-1)
    local animate = cc.Animate:create(animation)
    pterodactyl:runAction( animate )
    local moveOut = cc.MoveTo:create(0, cc.p(self.visibleSize.width
+ 100, self.visibleSize.height *
0.8))
    local moveIn = cc.MoveTo:create(4.0, cc.p(-100,
self.visibleSize.height * 0.8))
    local delay = cc.DelayTime:create(2.5)
pterodactyl:runAction(cc.RepeatForever:create
(cc.Sequence:create(moveOut, moveIn, delay) ) )
```

```
local character = cc.Sprite:create("introCharacter.png")
character:setPosition(self.middle.x, self.middle.y + 110)
self:addChild(character)
local frame = cc.Sprite:create("frame.png")
frame:setPosition(self.middle.x, self.middle.y)
self:addChild(frame)
end
```

With this, we added a background and two other sprites, plus an animation of a pterodactyl flying in the background. Once again, the calls are remarkably similar to the ones in C++.

5. Now let's add a menu with a play button (all this still inside the `init` method):

```
--create play button
local function playGame()
    local bgMusicPath =    cc.FileUtils:getInstance():fullPathForFi
lename("background.mp3")
    cc.SimpleAudioEngine:getInstance():playMusic(bgMusicPath, true)
    local scene = require("GameScene")
    local gameScene = scene.create()
    cc.Director:getInstance():replaceScene(gameScene)
end

local btnPlay = cc.MenuItemImage:create("playBtn.png",
"playBtnOver.png")
btnPlay:setPosition(0,0)
btnPlay:registerScriptTapHandler(playGame)
local menu  = cc.Menu:create(btnPlay)
menu:setPosition(self.middle.x, 80)
self:addChild(menu)
```

Typing the button's callback inside the same method where the callback is referenced is similar to writing a block or even a lambda function in C++.

What just happened?

You created a scene in Lua with Cocos2d-x using a menu, a few sprites, and an animation. It's easy to see how similar the calls are in the Lua bindings to the original C++ ones. And with code completion inside the IDE, finding the correct methods is a breeze.

Now let's tackle the GameScene class.

One of the nicest features of Lua is something called **live coding**, and it's switched on by default in the Cocos IDE. To see what I mean by live coding, do this: while the game is running in the simulator, change the position of the character sprite in your code and save it. You should see the change taking effect in the simulator. This is a great way to build UI and game scenes.

Time for action – creating our game scene

The `GameScene` class is already added to the start project and some of the code is already in place. We'll focus first on building the game's interface and listening to touches:

1. Let's work on the `addTouchEvents` method:

```lua
function GameScene:addTouchEvents()
    local bg = cc.Sprite:create("background.jpg")
    bg:setPosition(self.middle.x, self.middle.y)
    self:addChild(bg)

    local function onTouchBegan(touch, event)
        self.gridController:onTouchDown(touch:getLocation())
        return true
    end

    local function onTouchMoved(touch, event)
        self.gridController:onTouchMove(touch:getLocation())
    end

    local function onTouchEnded(touch, event)
        self.gridController:onTouchUp(touch:getLocation())
    end

    local listener = cc.EventListenerTouchOneByOne:create()
    listener:registerScriptHandler
(onTouchBegan,cc.Handler.EVENT_TOUCH_BEGAN )
    listener:registerScriptHandler
(onTouchMoved,cc.Handler.EVENT_TOUCH_MOVED )
    listener:registerScriptHandler
(onTouchEnded,cc.Handler.EVENT_TOUCH_ENDED )
    local eventDispatcher = bg:getEventDispatcher()
        eventDispatcher:addEventListenerWithSceneGraphPriority
(listener, bg)
end
```

2. Once again, we register the events with the node's instance of the event dispatcher. The actual touches are handled by our `GridController` object. We'll go over those later; first, let's build the UI. Time to work on the `init` method:

```lua
function GameScene:init ()
    self.gridController = GridController:create()
    self.gridAnimations = GridAnimations:create()
    self.objectPools = ObjectPools.create()

    self.gridAnimations:setGameLayer(self)
    self.gridController:setGameLayer(self)
    self.objectPools:createPools(self)
```

Create our special objects, one to handle user interactivity, another for animations, and our good old object pool.

3. Next, we add a couple of nodes and our score labels:

```lua
self:addChild( self.gemsContainer )
self.gemsContainer:setPosition( 25, 80)
--build interface
local frame = cc.Sprite:create("frame.png")
frame:setPosition(self.middle.x, self.middle.y)
self:addChild(frame)
local diamondScoreBg = cc.Sprite:create("diamondScore.png")
diamondScoreBg:setPosition(100, constants.SCREEN_HEIGHT - 30)
self:addChild(diamondScoreBg)
local scoreBg = cc.Sprite:create("gemsScore.png")
scoreBg:setPosition(280, constants.SCREEN_HEIGHT - 30)
self:addChild(scoreBg)
local ttfConfig = {}
ttfConfig.fontFilePath="fonts/myriad-pro.ttf"
ttfConfig.fontSize=20
self.diamondScoreLabel = cc.Label:createWithTTF(ttfConfig,
"0", cc.TEXT_ALIGNMENT_RIGHT , 150)
self.diamondScoreLabel:setPosition
(140, constants.SCREEN_HEIGHT - 30)
self:addChild(self.diamondScoreLabel)
self.scoreLabel = cc.Label:createWithTTF(ttfConfig,
"0", cc.TEXT_ALIGNMENT_RIGHT , 150)
self.scoreLabel:setPosition (330, constants.SCREEN_HEIGHT - 30)
self:addChild(self.scoreLabel)
end
```

The main difference when compared to the C++ implementation of `Label:createWithTTF` is that, in Lua, we have a configuration table for the font.

What just happened?

This time, we saw how to register for touch events and how to create true type font labels. Next, we'll go over creating a typical grid for a match-three game.

Time for action – building the gems

There are basically two types of match-three games, those in which the selection of matches takes place automatically and those in which the matches are selected by the player. *Candy Crush* is a good example of the former, and *Diamond Dash* of the latter. When building the first type of game, you must add extra logic to ensure you start the game with a grid that contains no matches. This is what we'll do now:

1. We start with the `buildGrid` method:

```
function GameScene:buildGrid ()
  math.randomseed(os.clock())
  self.enabled = false
  local g
  for c = 1, constants.GRID_SIZE_X do
      self.grid[c] = {}
      self.gridGemsColumnMap[c] = {}
      for r = 1, constants.GRID_SIZE_Y do
          if (c < 3) then
              self.grid[c][r] =
constants.TYPES[ self:getVerticalUnique(c,r) ]
          else
              self.grid[c][r] =
constants.TYPES[ self:getVerticalHorizontalUnique(c,r) ]
          end
          g = Gem:create()
          g:setType(  self.grid[c][r] )
          g:setPosition ( c * (constants.TILE_SIZE +
constants.GRID_SPACE),
              r * (constants.TILE_SIZE +
constants.GRID_SPACE))
          self.gemsContainer:addChild(g)
          self.gridGemsColumnMap[c][r] = g
          table.insert(self.allGems, g)
      end
  end
  self.gridAnimations:animateIntro()
end
```

Ensure that we generate a different random series of gems each time we run the game by changing the `randomseed` value.

The `enabled` property will stop user interactions while the grid is being altered or animated.

The grid is a two-dimensional array of columns of gems. The magic happens in the `getVerticalUnique` and `getVerticalHorizontalUnique` methods.

2. To ensure that none of the gems will form a three-gem-match on the first two columns, we check them vertically:

```
function GameScene:getVerticalUnique (col, row)
    local type = math.floor (math.random () *
#constants.TYPES + 1 )
    if (self.grid[col][row-1] == constants.TYPES[type] and
self.grid[col][row-2] ~= nil and self.grid[col][row-2] ==
constants.TYPES[type]) then
        type = type + 1;
        if (type == #constants.TYPES + 1) then type = 1 end
    end
    return type
end
```

All this code is doing is checking a column to see if any gem is forming a string of three connected gems of the same type.

3. Then, we check both vertically and horizontally, starting with column 3:

```
function GameScene:getVerticalHorizontalUnique (col, row)
    local type = self:getVerticalUnique (col, row)
    if (self.grid[col - 1][row] == constants.TYPES[type] and
self.grid[col - 2][row] ~= nil and self.grid[col - 2][row] ==
constants.TYPES[type]) then
        local unique = false
        while unique == false do
            type = self:getVerticalUnique (col, row)
            if (self.grid[col-1][row] == constants.TYPES[type] and
            self.grid[col - 2 ][row] ~= nil and  self.grid[col -
2 ][row] == constants.TYPES[type]) then
                --do nothing
            else
                unique = true
            end
        end
    end
    return type
end
```

This algorithm is doing the same thing we did previously with the columns, but it's also checking on individual rows.

What just happened?

We created a grid of gems, free of any three-gem matches. Again, if we had built the sort of match-three game where the user must select clusters of matched gems to have these removed from the grid (like *Diamond Dash*), we would not have to bother with this logic at all.

Next, let's manipulate the grid with gem swaps, identification of matches, and grid collapse.

Time for action – changing the grid with GridController

The `GridController` object initiates all grid changes since it's where we handle touches. In the game, the user can drag a gem to swap places with another, or first select the gem they want to move and then select the gem they want to swap places with in a two-touch process. Let's add the touch handling for that:

1. In `GridController`, let's add the logic to `onTouchDown`:

```
function GridController:onTouchDown (touch)
    if (self.gameLayer.running == false) then
        local scene = require("GameScene")
        local gameScene = scene.create()
        cc.Director:getInstance():replaceScene(gameScene)
        local bgMusicPath =
cc.FileUtils:getInstance():fullPathForFilename("background.mp3")
        cc.SimpleAudioEngine:getInstance():playMusic(bgMusicPath,
true)
        return
    end
```

    If we are displaying the game over screen, restart the scene.

2. Next, we find the gem the user is trying to select:

```
    self.touchDown = true
    if (self.enabled == false) then return end
    local touchedGem = self:findGemAtPosition (touch)
    if (touchedGem.gem ~= nil ) then
        if (self.gameLayer.selectedGem == nil) then
            self:selectStartGem (touchedGem)
        else
            if (self:isValidTarget (touchedGem.x,
touchedGem.y, touch) == true) then
                self:selectTargetGem (touchedGem)
            else
```

```
                    if (self.gameLayer.selectedGem ~= nil)
        then self.gameLayer.selectedGem:deselect() end
                    self.gameLayer.selectedGem = nil
                    self:selectStartGem (touchedGem)
            end
        end
    end
end
```

We find the gem closest to the touch position. If the user has not selected a gem yet (`selectedGem = nil`), we set the one just touched as the first gem selected. Otherwise, we determine whether the second gem selected can be used for a swap. Only gems above and below the first selected gem, or the ones to the left and right of it, can be swapped with. If that is valid, we use the second gem as the target gem.

3. Before moving on to `onTouchMove` and `onTouchUp`, let's see how we determine which gem is being selected and which gem is a valid target gem. So let's work on the `findGemAtPosition` value. Begin by determining where in the grid container the touch landed:

```
function GridController:findGemAtPosition (position)
    local mx = position.x
    local my = position.y
    local gridWidth = constants.GRID_SIZE_X *
(constants.TILE_SIZE + constants.GRID_SPACE)
    local gridHeight = constants.GRID_SIZE_Y *
(constants.TILE_SIZE + constants.GRID_SPACE)
    mx = mx - self.gameLayer.gemsContainer:getPositionX()
    my = my - self.gameLayer.gemsContainer:getPositionY()
    if (mx < 0) then mx = 0 end
    if (my < 0) then my = 0 end
    if (mx > gridWidth) then mx = gridWidth end
    if (my > gridHeight) then my = gridHeight end
```

4. Here is where the magic happens. We use the x and y position of the touch inside the grid to determine the index of the gem inside the array:

```
local x = math.ceil ((mx - constants.TILE_SIZE * 0.5) /
(constants.TILE_SIZE + constants.GRID_SPACE))
    local y = math.ceil ((my - constants.TILE_SIZE * 0.5) /
(constants.TILE_SIZE + constants.GRID_SPACE))
    if (x < 1) then x = 1 end
    if (y < 1) then y = 1 end
    if (x > constants.GRID_SIZE_X) then x =
constants.GRID_SIZE_X end
```

```
    if (y > constants.GRID_SIZE_Y) then y =
constants.GRID_SIZE_Y end
    return {x = x, y = y, gem =
self.gameLayer.gridGemsColumnMap[x][y] }
end
```

We finish by checking whether the touch is out of array bounds.

5. And now let's see the logic to determine whether the target gem is a valid target:

```
function GridController:isValidTarget (px, py, touch)
    local offbounds = false
    if (px > self.gameLayer.selectedIndex.x + 1) then
offbounds = true end
    if (px < self.gameLayer.selectedIndex.x - 1) then
offbounds = true end
    if (py > self.gameLayer.selectedIndex.y + 1) then
offbounds = true end
    if (py < self.gameLayer.selectedIndex.y - 1) then
offbounds = true end
```

We first check to see whether the target gem is at the top, bottom, left, or right of the selected gem:

```
local cell = math.sin (math.atan2
(math.pow( self.gameLayer.selectedIndex.x - px, 2),
math.pow( self.gameLayer.selectedIndex.y- py, 2) ) )
    if (cell ~= 0 and cell ~= 1) then
        offbounds = true
    end
    if (offbounds == true) then
        return false
    end
```

We next use a bit of trig magic to determine whether the selected target gem is diagonal to the selected gem:

```
    local touchedGem = self.gameLayer.gridGemsColumnMap[px][py]
    if (touchedGem.gem == self.gameLayer.selectedGem or
(px == self.gameLayer.selectedIndex.x and
py == self.gameLayer.selectedIndex.y)) then
        self.gameLayer.targetGem = nil
        return false
    end
    return true
end
```

We finish by checking whether the target gem is not the same as the previously selected gem.

6. Now, let's move on to the onTouchUp event handling:

```
function GridController:onTouchUp (touch)
    if (self.gameLayer.running == false) then return end
    self.touchDown = false
    if (self.enabled == false) then return end
    if (self.gameLayer.selectedGem ~= nil) then
self.gameLayer:dropSelectedGem() end
end
```

Pretty simple! We just change the z layering of the selected gem, as we want to make sure that the gem is shown above the others when the swap takes place. So when we release the gem, we push it back to its original z level (which is what the dropSelectedGem method does, and we'll see how it does this soon).

7. The onTouchMove event handles the option of dragging the selected gem until it swaps places with another gem:

```
function GridController:onTouchMove (touch)
    if (self.gameLayer.running == false) then return end
    if (self.enabled == false) then return end
    --track to see if we have a valid target
    if (self.gameLayer.selectedGem ~= nil and
self.touchDown == true) then
        self.gameLayer.selectedGem:setPosition(
        touch.x - self.gameLayer.gemsContainer:getPositionX(),
        touch.y - self.gameLayer.gemsContainer:getPositionY())
        local touchedGem = self:findGemAtPosition (touch)
        if (touchedGem.gem ~= nil and self:isValidTarget(touchedGe
m.x, touchedGem.y, touch) == true ) then
            self:selectTargetGem(touchedGem)
        end
    end
end
```

We run most of the same logic as we did with onTouchDown. We move the selectedGem object until a suitable target gem is identified, and then we pick the second one as the target. This is when the swap happens. Let's do that now.

8. First, the logic that sets our selected gem:

```
function GridController:selectStartGem (touchedGem)
      if (self.gameLayer.selectedGem == nil) then
        self.gameLayer.selectedGem = touchedGem.gem
        self.gameLayer.targetGem = nil
        self.gameLayer.targetIndex = nil
        touchedGem.gem:setLocalZOrder(constants.Z_SWAP_2)
        self.gameLayer.selectedIndex = {x = touchedGem.x,
y = touchedGem.y}
        self.gameLayer.selectedGemPosition =
{x = touchedGem.gem:getPositionX(),
                                            y =
touchedGem.gem:getPositionY()}
        self.gameLayer.gridAnimations:animateSelected
(touchedGem.gem)
    end
end
```

We start the swapping process; we have a selected gem but no target gem. We change the layering of the selected gem through `setLocalZOrder`. We also make the selected gem rotate 360 degrees.

9. Then, we're ready to select the target gem:

```
function GridController:selectTargetGem (touchedGem)
    if (self.gameLayer.targetGem ~= nil) then return end
    self.enabled = false
    self.gameLayer.targetIndex = {x = touchedGem.x,
y = touchedGem.y}
    self.gameLayer.targetGem = touchedGem.gem
    self.gameLayer.targetGem:setLocalZOrder(constants.Z_SWAP_1)
    self.gameLayer:swapGemsToNewPosition()
end
```

It is now that we finally call our `GameScene` class and ask it to swap the gems.

What just happened?

We just added the logic to handle all the user interactivity. Now, all that's left for us to do is handle the swaps, checking for matches and collapsing the grid. Let's do it!

Time for action – swapping the gems and looking for matches

The swapping logic is found in GameScene in the swapGemsToNewPosition method:

1. The swapGemsToNewPosition method makes one call to GridAnimations to animate the swap between the selected and target gem. Once this animation is complete, we fire a onNewSwapComplete method. The majority of the logic takes place in there:

```
function GameScene:swapGemsToNewPosition ()
    local function onMatchedAnimatedOut (sender)
        self:collapseGrid()
    end

    local function onReturnSwapComplete (sender)
        self.gridController.enabled = true
    end

    local function onNewSwapComplete (sender)
        self.gridGemsColumnMap[self.targetIndex.x][self.
targetIndex.y]
= self.selectedGem
        self.gridGemsColumnMap[self.selectedIndex.x][self.
selectedIndex.y] =
self.targetGem
        self.grid[self.targetIndex.x][self.targetIndex.y] =
self.selectedGem.type
        self.grid[self.selectedIndex.x][self.selectedIndex.y] =
self.targetGem.type
The call back switches the gems around inside the grid array.
        self.combos = 0
        self.addingCombos = true
Combos are used to track if we have more than 3 gems matched
after the player's move.
        --check for new matches
        if (self.gridController:checkGridMatches() == true) then
```

2. If we have a match, we run animations on the matched gems, otherwise we play a swap back animation and play a sound effect to represent a wrong move by the player:

```
            --animate matched gems
            if (#self.gridController.matchArray > 3) then
self.combos = self.combos + (#self.gridController.matchArray -
3) end
```

```
            self.gridAnimations:animateMatches
(self.gridController.matchArray, onMatchedAnimatedOut)
            self:showMatchParticle
(self.gridController.matchArray)
            self:setGemsScore(#self.gridController.matchArray *
constants.POINTS)
            self:playFX("match2.wav")
        else
            --no matches, swap gems back
            self.gridAnimations:swapGems (self.targetGem,
self.selectedGem, onReturnSwapComplete)
            self.gridGemsColumnMap[self.targetIndex.x][self.
targetIndex.y]
= self.targetGem
            self.gridGemsColumnMap[self.selectedIndex.x][self.
selectedIndex.y]
= self.selectedGem
            self.grid[self.targetIndex.x][self.targetIndex.y] =
self.targetGem.type
            self.grid[self.selectedIndex.x][self.selectedIndex.y]
=
self.selectedGem.type
            self:playFX("wrong.wav")
        end
```

At the end of each new animation, be it the match one or the swap back one, we once again run callbacks listed at the top of the method. The most important thing these do is the call to `collapseGrid` done when the matched gems finish animating inside the `onMatchedAnimatedOut` callback:

```
        self.selectedGem = nil
        self.targetGem = nil
    end
```

We end the callback by clearing the selected gems and start with a clean slate.

3. And here, at the end of the function, we call the swap gems animation with `onNewSwapComplete` as its callback:

```
    self.gridAnimations:swapGems (self.selectedGem, self.targetGem,
onNewSwapComplete)
end
```

4. Let's move back to `GridController` and add the `checkGridMatches` method. This is broken into three parts:

```lua
function GridController:checkGridMatches ()
    self.matchArray = {}
    for c = 1, constants.GRID_SIZE_X do
        for r = 1, constants.GRID_SIZE_Y do
            self:checkTypeMatch(c,r)
        end
    end
    if (#self.matchArray >= 2) then
        self.gameLayer:addToScore()
        return true
    end
    print("no matches")
    return false
end
```

This method starts the check by running `checkTypeMatch` on each cell.

5. The `checkTypeMatch` method searches around the current index and looks for matches at the top, bottom, left, and right of the index:

```lua
function GridController:checkTypeMatch (c, r)
    local type = self.gameLayer.grid[c][r]
    local stepC = c
    local stepR = r
    local temp_matches = {}
    --check top
    while stepR -1 >= 1 and self.gameLayer.grid[c][stepR-1] ==
type do
        stepR = stepR - 1
        table.insert (temp_matches, {x = c, y = stepR})
    end
    if (#temp_matches >= 2) then self:addMatches (temp_matches)
end
    temp_matches = {}
    --check bottom
    stepR = r
    while stepR + 1 <= constants.GRID_SIZE_Y
      and self.gameLayer.grid[c][stepR + 1] == type do
        stepR = stepR + 1
        table.insert (temp_matches, {x = c, y= stepR})
    end
```

```
        if (#temp_matches >= 2) then self:addMatches (temp_matches)
    end
        temp_matches = {}
        --check left
        while stepC - 1 >= 1 and self.gameLayer.grid[stepC - 1][r]
== type do
            stepC = stepC - 1
            table.insert (temp_matches, {x = stepC, y= r})
        end
        if (#temp_matches >= 2) then self:addMatches (temp_matches)
    end
        temp_matches = {}
        --check right
        stepC = c;
        while stepC + 1 <= constants.GRID_SIZE_X and
self.gameLayer.grid[stepC + 1][r] == type do
            stepC = stepC + 1
            table.insert (temp_matches, {x = stepC, y = r})
        end
        if (#temp_matches >= 2) then self:addMatches (temp_matches)
    end
    end
```

If any matches are found, they are added to the `matches` array.

6. But first we need to make sure there are no duplicates listed there, so when we
   add a gem to the `matches` array, we check whether it has not been added already:

```
function GridController:addMatches (matches)
    for key, value in pairs(matches) do
        if (self:find(value, self.matchArray) == false) then
            table.insert(self.matchArray, value)
        end
    end
end
```

7. And the simple method to look for duplicates:

```
function GridController:find (np, array)
    for key, value in pairs(array) do
        if (value.x == np.x and value.y == np.y) then return true
    end
    end
    return false
end
```

What just happened?

Finding matches is more than half the necessary logic for any match-three game. All you need to do is traverse the grid as effectively as you can and look for repeated patterns.

The rest of the logic concerns the grid collapse. We'll do that next and then we're ready to publish the game.

Time for action – collapsing the grid and repeating

So the flow of the game is move pieces around, look for matches, remove those, collapse the grid and add new gems, look for matches again, and if necessary, do the whole process in a loop:

1. This is the longest method in the game, and again, most of the logic happens inside callbacks. First we tag the gems being removed by setting their type data to -1. All the gems inside `matchArray` will be removed:

```
function GameScene:collapseGrid ()
    for i = 1, #self.gridController.matchArray do
        self.grid[self.gridController.matchArray[i].x]
        [self.gridController.matchArray[i].y] = -1
    end

    local column = nil
    local newColumn = nil
    local i
```

2. Next, we traverse the grid's columns and rearrange the gems whose type is not equal to -1 inside the column arrays. Essentially, we update the data here so that gems above the ones removed "fall down". The actual change will take place in the `animateCollapse` method:

```
    for c = 1, constants.GRID_SIZE_X do
        column = self.grid[c]
        newColumn = {}
        i = 1
        while #newColumn < #column do
            if (#column > i) then
                if (column[i] ~= -1) then
                    --move gem
                    table.insert(newColumn, column[i])
                end
            else
```

```
              --create new gem
              table.insert(newColumn, 1, column[i])
         end
         i = i+1
      end
      self.grid[c] = newColumn
   end
   self.gridAnimations:animateCollapse
(onGridCollapseComplete)
end
```

3. But now, let's code the callback of that animation called
`onGridCollapseComplete`. So above the code we've entered already inside
`collapseGrid`, we add the `local` function:

```
local function onGridCollapseComplete (sender)
   local function onMatchedAnimatedOut (sender)
      self:collapseGrid()
   end
   for i = 1, #self.allGems do
      local gem = self.allGems[i]
      local xIndex = math.ceil ((gem:getPositionX() -
constants.TILE_SIZE * 0.5) / (constants.TILE_SIZE +
constants.GRID_SPACE))
      local yIndex = math.ceil ((gem:getPositionY() -
constants.TILE_SIZE * 0.5) / (constants.TILE_SIZE +
constants.GRID_SPACE))
      self.gridGemsColumnMap[xIndex][yIndex] = gem
      self.grid[xIndex][yIndex] = gem.type
   end
```

First, we update the array of sprites, sorting them by the new x and y indexes
of the grid.

4. Then, we check for matches again. Remember that this callback runs after the grid
collapse animation has finished, which means new gems have been added already
and these may create new matches (we'll look at the logic soon):

```
if (self.gridController:checkGridMatches () == true) then
      --animate matched games
      if (self.addingCombos == true) then
         if (#self.gridController.matchArray > 3) then
self.combos = self.combos + (#self.gridController.matchArray -
3) end
      end
```

```
        self.gridAnimations:animateMatches
(self.gridController.matchArray, onMatchedAnimatedOut)
        self:showMatchParticle (self.gridController.matchArray)
        self:setGemsScore(#self.gridController.matchArray *
constants.POINTS)
        self:playFX("match.wav")
```

5. Then, if we find no more matches, we replace some random gems with diamonds if the value for combos is above 0 (meaning we had more than a 3 gem match in the last player's move):

```
else
    --no more matches, check for combos
    if (self.combos > 0) then
    --now turn random gems into diamonds
        local diamonds = {}
        local removeGems = {}
        local i = 0

        math.randomseed(os.clock())
        while i < self.combos do
          i = i + 1
          local randomGem = nil
          local randomX,randomY = 0
          while randomGem == nil do
             randomX = math.random(1, constants.GRID_SIZE_X)
             randomY = math.random(1, constants.GRID_SIZE_Y)
             randomGem = self.gridGemsColumnMap[randomX][randomY]
             if (randomGem.type == constants.TYPE_GEM_WHITE)
then randomGem = nil end
          end
```

6. And we pick random gems for the diamonds:

```
        local diamond = self.objectPools:getDiamond()
        diamond:setPosition(randomGem:getPositionX(),
randomGem:getPositionY())
        local diamondParticle =
self.objectPools:getDiamondParticle()
        diamondParticle:setPosition(randomGem:getPositionX(),
randomGem:getPositionY())
          table.insert(diamonds, diamond)
          table.insert(removeGems, {x=randomX, y=randomY})
        end
        self:setDiamondScore(#diamonds *
constants.DIAMOND_POINTS)
```

Animate the diamonds being collected, and at the end of that animation, call back onMatchedAnimatedOut, which will collapse the grid once more now that we had gems "burst" into diamonds:

```
        self.gridAnimations:animateMatches(removeGems,
onMatchedAnimatedOut)
      self.gridAnimations:collectDiamonds(diamonds)
      self.combos = 0
      self:playFX("diamond2.wav")
    else
      self.gridController.enabled = true
    end
      self.addingCombos = false
    end
end
```

7. Here's the whole `collapseGrid` method:

```
function GameScene:collapseGrid ()
    local function onGridCollapseComplete (sender)
        local function onMatchedAnimatedOut (sender)
            self:collapseGrid()
        end
        for i = 1, #self.allGems do
            local gem = self.allGems[i]
            local xIndex = math.ceil ((gem:getPositionX() -
constants.TILE_SIZE * 0.5) / (constants.TILE_SIZE +
constants.GRID_SPACE))
            local yIndex = math.ceil ((gem:getPositionY() -
constants.TILE_SIZE * 0.5) / (constants.TILE_SIZE +
constants.GRID_SPACE))
            self.gridGemsColumnMap[xIndex][yIndex] = gem
            self.grid[xIndex][yIndex] = gem.type
        end
        if (self.gridController:checkGridMatches () == true) then
            --animate matched games
            if (self.addingCombos == true) then
                if (#self.gridController.matchArray > 3) then
self.combos = self.combos + (#self.gridController.matchArray -
3) end
            end
            self.gridAnimations:animateMatches
(self.gridController.matchArray, onMatchedAnimatedOut)
            self:showMatchParticle
(self.gridController.matchArray)
```

```
            self:setGemsScore(#self.gridController.matchArray *
constants.POINTS)
            self:playFX("match.wav")
        else
            --no more matches, check for combos
            if (self.combos > 0) then
                --now turn random gems into diamonds
                local diamonds = {}
                local removeGems = {}
                local i = 0
                math.randomseed(os.clock())
                while i < self.combos do
                    i = i + 1
                    local randomGem = nil
                     local randomX,randomY = 0
                    while randomGem == nil do
                        randomX =
math.random(1, constants.GRID_SIZE_X)
                        randomY =
math.random(1, constants.GRID_SIZE_Y)
                        randomGem =
self.gridGemsColumnMap[randomX][randomY]
                        if (randomGem.type ==
constants.TYPE_GEM_WHITE) then randomGem = nil end
                    end
                    local diamond =
self.objectPools:getDiamond()
                        diamond:setPosition(randomGem:getPositionX(),
randomGem:getPositionY())
                        local diamondParticle =
self.objectPools:getDiamondParticle()
                        diamondParticle:setPosition(randomGem:getPosit
ionX(),
randomGem:getPositionY())
                    table.insert(diamonds, diamond)
                    table.insert(removeGems, {x=randomX,
y=randomY})
                end
                self:setDiamondScore(#diamonds *
constants.DIAMOND_POINTS)
                self.gridAnimations:animateMatches(removeGems,
onMatchedAnimatedOut)
                self.gridAnimations:collectDiamonds(diamonds)
                self.combos = 0
```

```
                        self:playFX("diamond2.wav")
                else
                    self.gridController.enabled = true
                end
                self.addingCombos = false
            end
        end
        for i = 1, #self.gridController.matchArray do
            self.grid[self.gridController.matchArray[i].x]
    [self.gridController.matchArray[i].y] = -1
        end

        local column = nil
        local newColumn = nil
        local i
        for c = 1, constants.GRID_SIZE_X do
            column = self.grid[c]
            newColumn = {}
            i = 1
            while #newColumn < #column do
                if (#column > i) then
                    if (column[i] ~= -1) then
                        --move gem
                        table.insert(newColumn, column[i])
                    end
                else
                    --create new gem
                    table.insert(newColumn, 1, column[i])
                end
                i = i+1
            end
            self.grid[c] = newColumn
        end
        self.gridAnimations:animateCollapse
    (onGridCollapseComplete)
    end
```

What just happened?

The collapseGrid method collects all the gems affected by matches or gems which exploded into diamonds. The resulting array is sent to GridAnimations for the proper animations to be performed.

We'll work on those next and finish our game.

Time for action – animating matches and collapses

Now for the last bit of logic: the final animations:

1. We'll start with the easy ones:

```lua
function GridAnimations:animateSelected (gem)
    gem:select()
    gem:stopAllActions()
    local rotate = cc.EaseBounceOut:create (
cc.RotateBy:create(0.5, 360) )
    gem:runAction(rotate)
end
```

This rotates a gem; we use this animation when a gem is first selected.

2. Next is the swap animation:

```lua
function GridAnimations:swapGems
(gemOrigin, gemTarget, onComplete)
    gemOrigin:deselect()
   local origin = self.gameLayer.selectedGemPosition
    local target = cc.p(gemTarget:getPositionX(),
gemTarget:getPositionY())
    local moveSelected =
cc.EaseBackOut:create(cc.MoveTo:create(0.8, target) )
    local moveTarget =
cc.EaseBackOut:create(cc.MoveTo:create(0.8, origin) )
    local callback = cc.CallFunc:create(onComplete)
   gemOrigin:runAction(moveSelected)
    gemTarget:runAction (cc.Sequence:create(moveTarget, callback))
end
```

All this does is swap the places of the first selected gem and the target gem.

3. Then, we add the animations we run for matched gems:

```lua
function GridAnimations:animateMatches (matches, onComplete)
    local function onCompleteMe (sender)
        self.animatedMatchedGems = self.animatedMatchedGems - 1;
        if (self.animatedMatchedGems == 0) then
            if (onComplete ~= nil) then onComplete() end
        end
end
    self.animatedMatchedGems = #matches
   local gem = nil
    for i, point in ipairs(matches) do
        gem = self.gameLayer.gridGemsColumnMap[point.x]
[point.y]
        gem:stopAllActions()
```

```
        local scale = cc.EaseBackOut:create
( cc.ScaleTo:create(0.3, 0))
        local callback = cc.CallFunc:create(onCompleteMe)
        local action = cc.Sequence:create (scale, callback)
        gem.gemContainer:runAction(action)
    end
end
```

This will scale down a gem to nothing, and only fire the final callback when all gems have finish scaling.

4. Next is the collect diamonds animation:

```
function GridAnimations:collectDiamonds(diamonds)
    local function removeDiamond (sender)
        sender:setVisible(false)
    end
    for i = 1, #diamonds do
        local delay = cc.DelayTime:create(i * 0.05)
        local moveTo = cc.EaseBackIn:create( cc.MoveTo:create
( 0.8, cc.p(50, constants.SCREEN_HEIGHT - 50) ) )
        local action = cc.Sequence:create
(delay, moveTo, cc.CallFunc:create(removeDiamond))
        diamonds[i]:runAction(action)
    end
end
```

This moves the diamonds to where the diamond score label is.

5. And now, finally, add the grid collapse:

```
function GridAnimations:animateCollapse ( onComplete )
    self.animatedCollapsedGems = 0
    local gem = nil
    local drop  = 1
  for c = 1, constants.GRID_SIZE_X do
        drop = 1
        for r = 1, constants.GRID_SIZE_Y do
            gem = self.gameLayer.gridGemsColumnMap[c][r]
            --if this gem has been resized, move it to the top
            if (gem.gemContainer:getScaleX() ~= 1) then
                gem:setPositionY((constants.GRID_SIZE_Y +
(drop)) * (constants.TILE_SIZE + constants.GRID_SPACE))
                self.animatedCollapsedGems =
self.animatedCollapsedGems + 1
                gem:setType ( self.gameLayer:getNewGem() )
                gem:setVisible(true)
                local newY = (constants.GRID_SIZE_Y -
(drop - 1)) * (constants.TILE_SIZE + constants.GRID_SPACE)
```

```
                                self:dropGemTo (gem, newY,  0.2, onComplete)
                                drop = drop + 1
                        else
                            if (drop > 1) then
                                self.animatedCollapsedGems =
        self.animatedCollapsedGems + 1
                                local newY = gem:getPositionY() -
        (drop - 1) * (constants.TILE_SIZE + constants.GRID_SPACE)
                                self:dropGemTo (gem, newY, 0, onComplete)
                            end
                    end
                end
            end
        end
```

We loop through all the gems and identify the ones that have been scaled down, meaning the ones which were *removed*. We move these above the column, so they will fall down as new gems, and we pick a new type for them:

```
gem:setType ( self.gameLayer:getNewGem() )
```

The ones which were not removed will drop to their new positions. The way we do this is simple. We count how many gems were removed until we reached a gem which has not been removed. That count is stored in the local variable drop, which is reset to 0 with every column.

That way, we know how many gems were removed below other gems. We use that to find the new y position.

6. The dropGemTo new position looks like this:

```
function GridAnimations:dropGemTo (gem, y, delay, onComplete)
        gem:stopAllActions()
    gem:reset()
    local function onCompleteMe  (sender)
        self.animatedCollapsedGems =
    self.animatedCollapsedGems - 1;
        if ( self.animatedCollapsedGems == 0 ) then
            if (onComplete ~= nil) then onComplete() end
        end
    end
    local move = cc.EaseBounceOut:create
(cc.MoveTo:create (0.6, cc.p(gem:getPositionX(), y) ) )
    local action = cc.Sequence:create
(cc.DelayTime:create(delay), move,
cc.CallFunc:create(onCompleteMe))
    gem:runAction(action)
end
```

Again, we only fire the final callback once all gems have collapsed. This final callback will run another check for matches, as we've seen earlier, starting the whole process again.

What just happened?

That's it; we have the three main parts of a match-three game: the swap, the matches, and the collapse.

There is only one animation we haven't covered, which is already included in the code for this chapter, and that is the column drop for the intro animation when the grid is first created. But there's nothing new with that one. Feel free to review it, though.

Now, it's time to publish the game.

Time for action – publishing the game with the Cocos IDE

In order to build and publish the game, we'll need to tell the IDE a few things. I'll show you how to publish the game for Android, but the steps are very similar for any of the other targets:

1. First, let's tell the IDE where to find the Android SDK, NDK, and ANT, just as we did when we installed the Cocos2d-x console. In the IDE, open the **Preferences** panel. Then, under **Cocos**, enter the three paths just like we did before (remember that for ANT, you need to navigate to its `bin` folder).

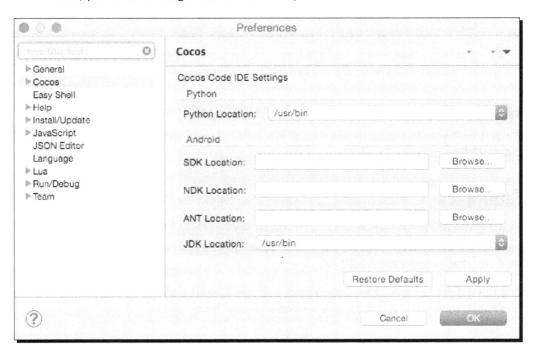

2. Now, in order to build the project, you need to select the fourth button at the top of the IDE (from the left-hand side), or right-click on your project and select **Cocos Tools**. You'll have different options available depending on which stage you are at in the deployment process.

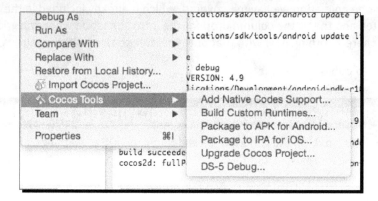

First, the IDE needs to add the native code support, and then it builds the project inside a folder called frameworks (it will contain an iOS, Mac OS, Windows, Android, and Linux version of your project just as if you had created it through the Cocos console).

3. You can then choose to package the application into an APK or IPA, which you can transfer to your phone. Or, you can use the generated project inside Eclipse or Xcode.

What just happened?

You just built your Lua game to Android, or iOS, or Windows, or Linux, or Mac OS, or all of them! Well done.

Summary

That's it. You can now choose between C++ or Lua to build your games. The whole API can be accessed either way. So, every game created in this book can be done in either language (and yes, that includes the Box2D API.)

And this is it for the book. I hope you're not too tired to start working on your own ideas. And I hope to see your game sometime soon in an App Store near me!

Vector Calculations with Cocos2d-x

This appendix will cover some of the math concepts used in *Chapter 5, On the Line – Rocket Through*, in a little more detail.

What are vectors?

First, let's do a quick refresh on vectors and the way you can use Cocos2d-x to deal with them.

So what is the difference between a vector and a point? At first, they seem to be the same. Consider the following point and vector:

- Point (2, 3.5)
- Vec2 (2, 3.5)

The following figure illustrates a point and a vector:

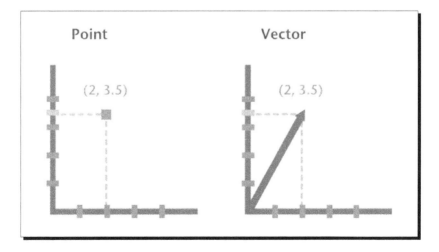

In this figure, they each have the same value for *x* and *y*. So what's the difference?

With a vector, you always have extra information. It is as if, besides those two values for *x* and *y*, we also have the *x* and *y* of the vector's origin, which in the previous figure we can assume to be point (0, 0). So the vector is *moving* in the direction described from point (0, 0) to point (2, 3.5). The extra information we can derive then from vectors is direction and length (usually referred to as magnitude).

It's as if a vector is a person's stride. We know how long each step is, and we know the direction in which the person is walking.

In game development, vectors can be used, among other things, to describe movement (speed, direction, acceleration, friction, and so on) or the combining forces acting upon a body.

The vector methods

There is a lot you can do with vectors, and there are many ways to create them and manipulate them. And Cocos2d-x comes bundled with helper methods that will take care of most of the calculations for you. Here are some examples:

- You have a vector, and you want to get its angle—use `getAngle()`
- You want the length of a vector—use `getLength()`
- You want to subtract two vectors; for example, to reduce the amount of movement of a sprite by another vector—use `vector1 - vector2`
- You want to add two vectors; for example, to increase the amount of movement of a sprite by another vector—use `vector1 + vector2`
- You want to multiply a vector; for example, applying a friction value to the amount of movement of a sprite—use `vector1 * vector2`
- You want the vector that is perpendicular to another (also known as a vector's normal)—use `getPerp()` or `getRPerp()`
- And, most importantly for our game example, you want the dot product of two vectors—use `dot(vector1, vector2)`

Now let me show you how to use these methods in our game example.

Using ccp helper methods

In the example of *Rocket Through*, the game we developed in *Chapter 5, On the Line – Rocket Through*, we used vectors to describe movement, and now I want to show you the logic behind some of the methods we used to handle vector operations and what they mean.

Rotating the rocket around a point

Let's start, as an example, with the rocket sprite moving with a vector of (5, 0):

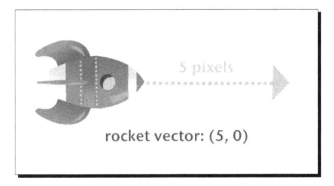

We then draw a line from the rocket, say from point **A** to point **B**:

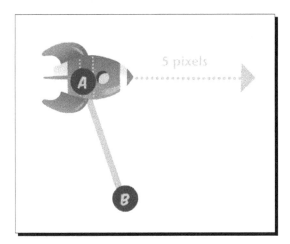

Now we want the rocket to rotate around point **B**. So how can we change the rocket's vector to accomplish that? With Cocos2d-x, we can use the helper point method rotateByAngle to rotate a point around any other point. In this case, we rotate the rocket's position point around point **B** by a certain angle.

But here's a question – in which direction should the rocket rotate?

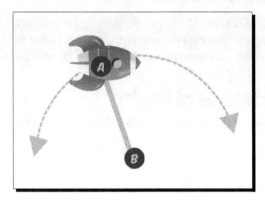

By looking at this figure, you know that the rocket should rotate clockwise, since it's moving towards the right. But programmatically, how could we determine that, and in the easiest way possible? We can determine this by using vectors and another property derived from them: the dot product.

Using the dot product of vectors

The dot product of two vectors describes their angular relationship. If their dot product is greater than zero, the two vectors form an angle smaller than 90 degrees. If it is less than zero, the angle is greater than 90 degrees. And if it is equal to zero, the vectors are perpendicular. Have a look at this descriptive figure:

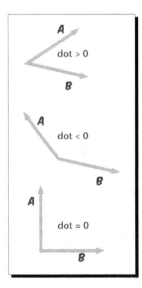

But one other way to think about this is that if the dot product is a positive value, then the vectors will "point" in the same direction. If it is a negative value, they point in opposite directions. How can we use that to help us?

A vector will always have two perpendiculars, as shown in the following figure:

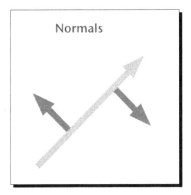

These perpendiculars are often called right and left, or clockwise and counterclockwise perpendiculars, and they are themselves vectors, known as normals.

Now, if we calculate the dot product between the rocket's vector and each of the perpendiculars on line **AB**, you can see that we can determine the direction the rocket should rotate in. If the dot product of the rocket and the vector's right perpendicular is a positive value, it means the rocket is moving towards the right (clockwise). If not, it means the rocket is moving towards the left (counterclockwise).

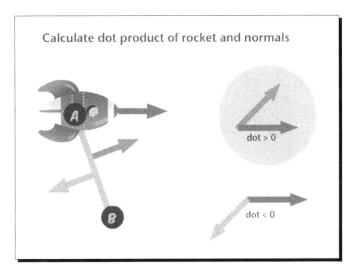

The dot product is very easy to calculate. We don't even need to bother with the formula (though it's a simple one), because we can use the `dot(vector1, vector2)` method.

So we have the vector for the rocket already. How do we get the vector for the normals? First, we get the vector for the **AB** line. We use another method for this – `point1 - point2`. This will subtract points **A** and **B** and return a vector representing that line.

Next, we can get the left and right perpendiculars of that line vector with the `getPerp()` and `getRPerp()` methods respectively. However, we only need to check one of these. Then we get the dot product with `dot(rocketVector, lineNormal)`.

If this is the correct normal, meaning the value for the dot product is a positive one, we can rotate the rocket to point to this normal's direction; so the rocket will be at a 90-degree angle with the line at all times as it rotates. This is easy, because we can convert the normal vector to an angle with the `getAngle()` method. All we need to do is apply that angle to the rocket.

But how fast should the rocket rotate? We'll see how to calculate that next.

Moving from pixel-based speed to angular-based speed

When rotating the rocket, we still want to show it moving at the same speed as it was when moving in a straight line, or as close to it as possible. How do we do that?

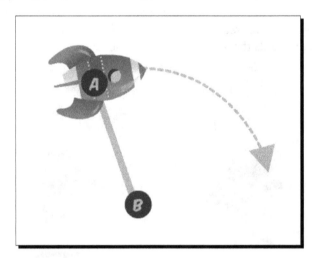

Remember that the vector is being used to update the rocket's position in every iteration. In the example I gave you, the (5, 0) vector is currently adding 5 pixels to the x position of the rocket in every iteration.

Now let's consider an angular speed. If the angular speed were 15 degrees, and we kept rotating the rocket's position by that angle, it would mean the rocket would complete a full circle in 24 iterations. Because 360 degrees of a full circle divided by 15 degrees equals 24.

But we don't have the correct angle yet; we only have the amount in pixels the rocket moves in every iteration. But math can tell us a lot here.

Math says that the length of a circle is *twice the value of Pi, multiplied by the radius of the circle*, usually written as *2πr*.

We know the radius of the circle we want the rocket to describe. It is the length of the line we drew.

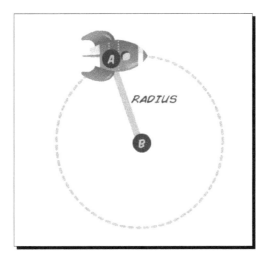

With that formula, we can get the length in pixels of that circle, also known as its circumference. Let's say the line has a length of 100 pixels; this would mean the circle about to be described by the rocket has a length (or circumference) of 628.3 pixels (2 * π * 100).

With the speed described in the vector (5, 0), we can determine how long it would take the rocket to complete that pixel length. We don't need this to be absolutely precise; the last iteration will most likely move beyond that total length, but it's good enough for our purposes.

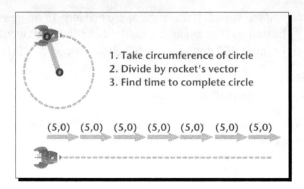

When we have the total number of iterations to complete the length, we can convert that to an angle. So, if the iteration value is 125, the angle would be 360 degrees divided by 125; that is, 2.88. That would be the angle required to describe a circle in 125 iterations.

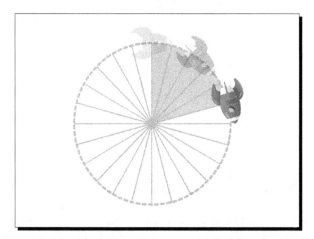

Now the rocket can change from pixel-based movement to angular-based movement without much visual change.

B
Pop Quiz Answers

Chapter 4, Fun with Sprites – Sky Defense

Pop quiz – sprites and actions

Q1	2
Q2	1
Q3	3
Q4	4

Chapter 8, Getting Physical – Box2D

Pop quiz

Q1	3
Q2	2
Q3	1
Q4	3

Index

Thank you for buying
Cocos2d-x by Example Beginner's Guide
Second Edition

About Packt Publishing

Packt, pronounced 'packed', published its first book, *Mastering phpMyAdmin for Effective MySQL Management*, in April 2004, and subsequently continued to specialize in publishing highly focused books on specific technologies and solutions.

Our books and publications share the experiences of your fellow IT professionals in adapting and customizing today's systems, applications, and frameworks. Our solution-based books give you the knowledge and power to customize the software and technologies you're using to get the job done. Packt books are more specific and less general than the IT books you have seen in the past. Our unique business model allows us to bring you more focused information, giving you more of what you need to know, and less of what you don't.

Packt is a modern yet unique publishing company that focuses on producing quality, cutting-edge books for communities of developers, administrators, and newbies alike. For more information, please visit our website at www.packtpub.com.

About Packt Open Source

In 2010, Packt launched two new brands, Packt Open Source and Packt Enterprise, in order to continue its focus on specialization. This book is part of the Packt Open Source brand, home to books published on software built around open source licenses, and offering information to anybody from advanced developers to budding web designers. The Open Source brand also runs Packt's Open Source Royalty Scheme, by which Packt gives a royalty to each open source project about whose software a book is sold.

Writing for Packt

We welcome all inquiries from people who are interested in authoring. Book proposals should be sent to author@packtpub.com. If your book idea is still at an early stage and you would like to discuss it first before writing a formal book proposal, then please contact us; one of our commissioning editors will get in touch with you.

We're not just looking for published authors; if you have strong technical skills but no writing experience, our experienced editors can help you develop a writing career, or simply get some additional reward for your expertise.

Cocos2d-x Game Development Essentials

ISBN: 978-1-78398-786-3   Paperback: 136 pages

Create iOS and Android games from scratch
using Cocos2d-x

1. Create and run Cocos2d-x projects on iOS and
   Android platforms.

2. Find practical solutions to many real-world game
   development problems.

3. Learn the essentials of Cocos2d-x by writing code
   and following step-by-step instructions.

Learning Cocos2d-JS Game Development

ISBN: 978-1-78439-007-5   Paperback: 188 pages

Learn to create robust and engaging cross-platform
HTML5 games using Cocos2D-JS

1. Create HTML5 games running both on desktop
   and mobile devices, played with both mouse and
   touch controls.

2. Add advanced features such as realistic physics,
   particle effects, scrolling, tweaking, sound effects,
   background music, and more to your games.

3. Build exciting cross-platform games and build
   a memory game, an endless runner and a
   physics-driven game.

Please check **www.PacktPub.com** for information on our titles

www.ingramcontent.com/pod-product-compliance
Lightning Source LLC
Chambersburg PA
CBHW060532060326
40690CB00017B/3459